ANCESTRAL
VOICES

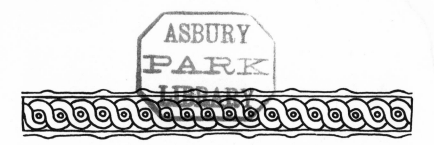

ANCESTRAL VOICES

Decoding Ancient Languages

by James Norman

Four Winds Press New York

Library of Congress Cataloging in Publication Data
Norman, James.
   Ancestral voices.
   Bibliography: p.
   1. Extinct languages.   2. Inscriptions—History.
3. Writing—History.   I. Title.
P901.N6   417′.7   75–14426
ISBN 0–590–17333–2

Published by Four Winds Press
A Division of Scholastic Magazines, Inc., New York, N.Y.
Copyright © 1975 by James Norman Schmidt

Printed in the United States of America
Library of Congress Catalog Card Number: 75–14426
   1   2   3   4   5   79   78   77   76   75

*And what there is to conquer . . . has already been
    discovered
Once or twice or several times . . .
There is only the fight to recover what has been lost
And found and lost again and again.*

—T. S. Eliot

*From the past let us take over the fire,
not the ashes.*

—Jean Jaurès

SEA

CASPIAN SEA

SYRIA

Carchemish

Khorsabad

Ninevah

Mosul

PERSIA
(IRAN)

Ras
Shamra

Nimrud

TIGRIS R.

MESOPOTAMIA

Behistun
Rock

Hamath

EUPHRATES

Damascas

RIVER

Bagdad

Susa

Babylon

Nippur

IRAQ

Ur

Persepolis

ARABIA

PERSIAN GULF

THE NEAR EAST

ANCESTRAL
VOICES

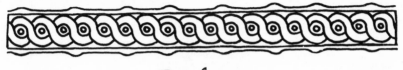

Preface

A little more than a century ago most educated men and women in America and Europe firmly believed that the roots of our Western civilization extended back no further than to ancient Greece and Palestine. Our philosophies, our arts and our sciences began with the Greeks; our religious traditions were shaped by the Hebrews. The tales told by Homer and the books of the Old Testament stood as the gateway between recorded history and the darkness of Western man's prehistory.

If anyone had suggested to our great-great-grandfathers that someone in Mesopotamia had written about a great deluge a thousand years before the story of Noah and his ark became part of our Biblical scripture, or if the same person had insisted that Homer's Troy really existed, he would have been called a crackpot. But today, thanks to our modern sciences, we have learned so much about mankind's early history that we no longer close our eyes or minds to startling ideas which would have been ridiculed a few generations ago. We accept the fact that Greece, Rome and Palestine were not the sole cradles of our cultural traditions, and we are aware that other ancient civilizations, tucked away and forgotten in Africa, Asia and the Americas, may have affected us, too.

When respected scholars at American universities and European institutes suggest that there might have been links between the writings of pre-Columbian Indians in the Americas and inhabitants of the Aegean world some thirty-five hundred years ago, hardly an eyebrow is raised. No one says, "Crackpot!" Although many experts may disagree with such an interesting hypothesis (to be discussed in our last chapter), the idea, nevertheless, is entertained in scientific circles. One of the reasons for this change in attitude is the development of a new science—literary archaeology.

Literary archaeology has to do with the quest of ancestral voices —messages from the past which were cut in stone, stamped on clay tablets, etched in bone, or drawn on papyrus sheets and animal skins. It includes the search for, the study of, and the decipherment of ancient writing. Although it is a fairly young science, scarcely a hundred years old, its students have already added more than two thousand years to the recorded history of Western civilization as well as recovering the rich histories and literatures of civilizations that were lost for centuries.

Unlike the physical archaeologist who studies the material remains of early man and ancient civilizations, thus revealing only the mute evidence of the past, the literary archaeologist focuses his attention on those societies in which man found a need to write. By locating and deciphering forgotten systems of writing, he gives the past a voice. He rescues ancient cultures from the abyss of time by turning back the pages of history so we not only learn what our ancestors felt and thought, but we discover how their ways and thoughts influence us today.

Although there are numerous books about the decipherment of forgotten scripts, for the most part they are quite technical, stressing the role that philology, linguistics, cryptanalysis and other studies have played in the recovery of ancient languages. The aim of this book, in addition to explaining as simply as possible how many "lost" languages were decoded, is to tell about the men who traveled across searing deserts, scaled impossible cliffs, or cut paths through dense jungles to salvage fragments of sentences or words which, when pieced together, helped rescue neglected empires from oblivion. The quest of ancestral scripts is also an intriguing detective story in which adventurers, explorers and scholars followed incredible hunches in order to solve mysteries that once seemed quite insoluble.

An example of such brilliant detectivelike deduction is one which occurred when students of the Assyrian-Babylonian cuneiforms began to speculate that this curious wedge-shaped writing was too complex to have been developed in a short time span by the Semitic-speaking people of Babylon and Assyria. It was suggested that the form of writing had been invented by an earlier, non-Semitic-speaking civilization. But which civilization? Explorers and archaeologists had scoured the Mesopotamian region and adjoining lands without turning up one shred of evidence revealing the existence of an earlier non-Semitic culture. Nevertheless, two scholars confidently predicted one would be found. One of them even gave the mysterious people a name—Sumerians. Then, years later, Sumer was found. Since then various Sumerian cities have been uncovered; Sumerian libraries have been located, and Sumerian histories and epics have been deciphered and translated into dozens of modern languages.

Though credit for important breakthroughs in the decipherment of ancient languages may sometimes be given to one person, in most cases the recovery of a forgotten script and the unfolding of a civilization's hidden history has usually been the result of international cooperation. The decipherer draws heavily on the expert knowledge of anthropologists, archaeologists, linguists, geologists, astronomers, historians, artists and physicists. Even the man or woman who compiles statistics or feeds data into an electronic computer assists the present-day decipherer who is still grappling with a score of ancient scripts which stubbornly refuse to give up their secrets.

This book, too, is the result of similar, though less technical, international cooperation. The author is deeply indebted to the following institutions and individuals whose research facilities, assistance, advice and guidance has made this work possible.

The British Museum, London; the Ashmolean Museum, Oxford; the National Museum of Anthropology, Mexico; the Library of Congress, Washington, D.C.; the Museum of Archaeology and History, Athens, Greece; the Heraklion Museum, Crete; the Peabody Museum at Harvard University; Ohio University Library.

For individual assistance and advice: Dr. Cyrus H. Gordon, Brandeis University; Ms. Francie Goldberg Robbins, Washington, D.C.; Dr. Stylianos Alexiou, Crete; Doctors Robert Ingham and Edgar Whan, Ohio University; Dr. Paul Schmidt, University of the Americas, Mexico; Dr. Tatiana Proskouriakoff, Harvard University; Mr. Innes Rose, London. For photographic assistance: Col. W. D. Barr and Dr. George G. Cameron, University of Michigan.

1

The Invention of Writing

Man has resided on earth for more than a million years, yet we know very little about how he lived or what he thought during most of this time. It is known, however, that in the Neolithic Era (late Stone Age) human communities and languages began to multiply in Europe, the Near East and Africa. In Africa alone some six hundred different tongues were spoken by various tribes and clans at least seven thousand years ago. In some of these societies the spoken tongue must have become quite expressive, capable of conveying a wide range of man's thoughts and intellectual achievements. But because sounds fade quickly, and words, though stored in the memory, are not safe from distortion, hundreds of these languages disappeared without leaving any trace behind. We have no idea what they were like because the speakers had no way of recording them for future generations. It is as if the people and their languages had never existed.

One of the most important factors in the rise of both ancient and modern civilizations was the development of writing. It has been called man's most revolutionary invention. Without it man could hardly have reached beyond the borders of his community or the frontiers of his mind.

The existence of great political empires such as that of Alexander the Great or of the Roman emperors would be hard to visualize if they had had no system of writing to bridge immense distances. Without some way to distribute information, military orders, and laws, the widely separated sections of the empire would have quickly fallen apart. So also, the great empires of the spirit and the mind, the religiocultural communities of the Roman Catholic Church and of Islam each depended on a written script to create a sense of religious solidarity. The Latin of the Catholic Church linked communities throughout the world. The Arabic script helped maintain the Mohammedan creed in North Africa and Pakistan, and among the Malayans as well as among the Swahili and Hausa Negroes of Africa.

The written word not only conveys man's languages and ideas across space but also across time. Without writing skills man could not have recorded his own reflections, his musings and his discoveries, passing them on from generation to generation. Only in writing has the rich and useful store of mankind's philosophies, literatures, religions and sciences been preserved with some fidelity. One can imagine how distorted a play by Shakespeare or Einstein's theory of relativity would become if they had not been written but simply passed from generation to generation by word of mouth.

Freezing spoken words into written form is a fairly modern invention, although there are suggestions that this accomplishment may be much older than we generally imagine. Most historians and anthropologists have maintained that man's ability to record simple ideas went back no further than ten thousand years ago. A few daring scholars, however, now think that some of our ancestors may have tinkered with a kind of prewriting long before the appearance of Neanderthal Man.

Recently, François Bordes of the University of Bordeaux uncovered an unusual ox rib while excavating in the rich archaeological region of Dordogne, France. Upon the rib a prehistoric man had engraved a series of curious signs—arcs, branches, angular symbols and parallel lines. Working with this material, Alexander Marshack, a research fellow at Harvard's Peabody Museum of Archaeology and Ethnology, stunned the scientific world with his analysis of these signs. Microscopic investigation revealed that the incisions on the bone were made over an extended period of time with various tools. Marshack has interpreted the symbols as time signs, suggesting that the prehistoric man kept a time record of the seasonal changes in nature, the fall of rain, the rise and fall of rivers, and the phases of the moon.

This theory is staggering because carbon 14 dating has set the age of the bone and its inscription at approximately 135,000 years ago. In other words, during an early ice age a primitive man in France seemed intelligent enough to devise complicated images and symbols in order to keep a record. Marshack's assumption has aroused much controversy among scientists, of course, and a good deal of time may pass before his idea is finally accepted or rejected.

Whether early man attempted to record ideas more than 135,000 years ago or only 10,000 years ago does not really affect our story of writing and decipherment, because these prehistoric attempts at communication belong more to the field of art history than to the history of writing. They do illustrate, however, how many forms of writing began.

Thousands of years before the invention of true writing men were depicting events in their lives with drawings called *pictograms*. These might be as simple as a wavy line to convey the idea of water, or the drawing might be more elaborate, perhaps the picture of a man holding a spear and a bison placed nearby to suggest a hunt. Such figures painted on rock are called *petrograms*; if they were carved in rock they are called *petroglyphs*.

The most famous petrograms are the handsome Altamira cave paintings discovered in Northern Spain in 1879 by the five-year-old daughter of the Marquis de Sautuola. While exploring the low-ceilinged cavern the Marquis had to crawl on his hands and knees, but his daughter, owing to her small size, was able to stand, stroll about, and look at the ceiling illuminated by her candle. Suddenly she cried out, *Toros! Toros, papá!* ("Bulls! Bulls, daddy!"). She had spied a life-size bison and other figures which had been painted by primitive men with rich mineral and earth colors. Since then the debris has been cleared from the cavern floor so that present-day visitors can stand up while admiring the story of an emotional hunt which was "written" more than 20,000 years ago.

Although each pictogram is simply a picture of some object—a man, the sun, an animal, a plant—a series of them, strung together, could tell a story; the pictures could correspond to a sentence or a longer narrative. A "reader" of such a message might interpret its story or meaning even if he did not know the spoken language of the artist.

The next step in pictorial writing was the development of the *ideogram*, a more sophisticated use of the pictogram. A true pictogram is an image of something that can be seen or touched, whereas when it is used as an ideogram some general idea or abstract concept is added. For example, a circle with rays projecting from it might depict the sun, but if it is used as an ideogram it might also represent bright light, warmth or some other attribute of the sun. A roadside sign with a picture of a tractor upon it merely indicates a tractor; when an X sign is drawn over the figure of the tractor it becomes an ideogram saying, "No tractors allowed on the pavement."

Converting pictograms into ideograms requires general agreement on the part of a clan or society to accept the additional meanings. It also demands a little more imagination and intelligence on the part of the "reader." It became the first real advance toward conventional writing. Ideograms played an important role in Egyptian hieroglyphics, one of the world's first major writing systems. The hieroglyphic pictogram showing an old, bent-over man leaning on a staff originally meant nothing more than "old man," but eventually it came to mean "aging," "decrepit" or "to lean upon" more than it signified an old man.

Although pictograms and ideograms are ages old, they are still used in modern-day communications. They are quickly understood and are especially useful in situations where a traveler may not understand the language of another country. Throughout the world the silhouette of a man on a restroom door plainly says, "The use of this room is for men only." Highway signs with similar pictures of a skidding automobile, a cow or two running children tell us, "Slippery when wet," "Cattle crossing or beware of cattle" and "Slow down, school."

As people became busier some of them found a need to simplify their writing. Rather than tediously draw the figure of a man or woman a scribe might devise a symbol such as this φ to indicate a human being. This was another useful shorthand step in the evolution of writing. Such a sign could be used to express a very complex bit of information. In Hans Jensen's monumental survey of writing, *Sign, Symbol and Script*, there is a vivid example of Nsibidi writing using the above sign. When the Ibos of Nigeria wish to say a husband and wife are quarreling they write ⟆ . The signs for man and woman are placed in a horizontal position, as though husband and wife were lying in bed, back to back. A stick or barrier is placed between them.

As writing developed, pictographic images often became symbols. These were sometimes picked up by other people who were shaping their own systems. Occasionally these evolved into signs standing for a letter, syllable or sound. The common pictograph for water ⌇ , or the Egyptian ideograph for water and water activities ⋀⋀ , went through some of the following variations before it became our letter *M*.

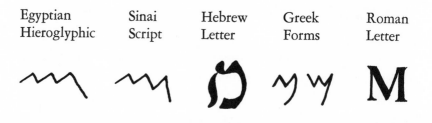

Egyptian Hieroglyphic	Sinai Script	Hebrew Letter	Greek Forms	Roman Letter

Pictorial images, even when reduced to symbols, may be very expressive, but as systems of writing they had two serious faults. First, there was never any connection between the drawn figure and the sound of the spoken language. Such images could only represent concrete things or, in a limited way, express a few abstract ideas. Second, pictography is unwieldly and time-consuming. As civilizations grew and men's activities and thoughts became more complex, their spoken language far outstripped what could be communicated by pictures. Thus the need for a more precise, less clumsy mode of writing developed.

A step in this direction was taken by the Egyptians when they utilized homonyms. These are graphic signs or words which look the same yet serve several purposes. Our word *pool* can mean "pool of water" or a "game of pool." In Egyptian hieroglyphics it was possible for an ideograph to do duty not only for the object pictured but for all its homonyms. The hieroglyphic sign for "lotus" was a pictograph of a lotus flower ⚘ . It was called or pronounced *kha.* As a homonym it also stood for the numeral 1,000. At the same time, the sign for "finger" ⋂ also stood for the numeral 10,000. The sign for a cow or cattle was the pictograph 🐄 . Thus in order to write "25,000 head of cattle" the Egyptian scribe painstakingly combined a pictograph with pictograph-homonyms in this manner:

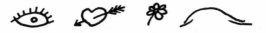

Yes, a clumsy method of writing, but at least sounds were being attached to the signs: *kha* for "lotus" and for "1,000"; *djeba* for "finger" and for "10,000." This evolutionary step is what scholars call the phoneticization of writing.

Another step along this route is the rebus principle used in many ancient languages. A rebus allows people to compose abstract ideas while still using pictograms. For example, string together the pictogram for an eye, the ideogram symbol for love, the pictograms for a daisy and a hill:

Aloud, it reads, "I love Daisy Hill." Similarly one might draw a picture of a nondescript dog followed by a picture of a tail; combined they express the verb *curtail.*

Once man began linking a single sign to a single sound, regardless of the visual meaning, he was taking the most important step toward phonetic writing, that is, toward recording the sounds of his spoken language. The process was often a slow one. For centuries the Egyptian hieroglyph ⬭ simply represented lips or a mouth, then it began to stand for the sound *rē*, meaning "mouth," and much later it was employed for a single sound *r*, in any context. When this happens writing becomes easier and there is less fuzziness in its meanings.

Even when they become phonetic, not all written languages develop in the same way. Some tongues that have numerous monosyllabic words as well as fairly simple polysyllabic words may use a sign or a letter that will stand for an entire syllable. For example, the Minoan Linear B script, employed by a race of compulsive bookkeepers long before Homer's time, had eighty-seven different signs representing syllable sounds.

Some of the 87 Linear B syllabic sounds and their signs

da	di	de	du	dwe	te	to	ti	ta

Such languages are called *syllabic*. It would appear that a syllabary system of writing should be easy to manage, but this is not always true, because too many signs become difficult to read at a glance.

Among the four hundred kinds of writing, a small number of them, instead of becoming syllabic, developed a simpler sound-to-symbol relationship in which each sound is represented by a letter sign. These languages are called alphabetic. Although the alphabetic systems appear to be the ultimate stage in language evolution, they are still not perfect. No really pure phonetic writing has yet come into use. Many of our highly refined European languages fail to record spoken sounds with absolute accuracy. English is noteworthy for containing a large number of words in which the written form hardly seems related to the spoken sound. Shouldn't the word *laugh* be written *laff?* Why is the English county of *Worcestershire* always pronounced *Wooster?*

Up to this point we have given a simplified account of the evolution of writing based on the generally accepted idea that the recording of languages throughout the world began with pictorial representations of concrete things or ideograms depicting a few abstract ideas, then these gradually evolved into symbolic signs which, in some cases, abandoned their pictorial function and stood for sounds. Today, however, some historians of languages feel that in some regions the phonetic letter or sign existed at the very onset of writing. There is some evidence that the prehistoric Anatolians in the highlands of Turkey, the primitive Alpine people of Europe and the prehistoric Iberians of Spain may have discovered and attached signs to isolated sounds at the same time, or before, the Greeks adopted and adapted the Phoenician alphabet for their use.

The shaping of signs to sounds was not the only thing to affect the form of scripts. The signs and symbols men used to record their thoughts or speech have often been modified by the writing tools and materials they had at hand. An illustration of this is the changes in Egyptian writing over tens of centuries. The earliest hieroglyphs were carved on stone monuments. The material used (stone) and the tools (hammer and chisel) dictated the shape and size of the writing—pictorial signs which were usually quite large. Centuries later this lumbering, artistic kind of writing was replaced by the Egyptian hieratic script, mainly because the scribes wrote with ink and a fine brush on papyrus paper. Thus the writing became smaller and finer and flowed swiftly. The shape of the signs looked less like the original pictogram from which they sprang; they almost began to resemble letters. Still later the demotic form of the script was developed. It was a simpler, more popular form derived from the hieratic style.

Changes in the forms of Egyptian writing

| Hieroglyph | Hieratic | Demotic |
| 2000 B.C. | 1300 B.C. | 300–100 B.C. |

Technological advances such as the invention of paper and the refinement of writing tools were not the only things to change the forms of writing. The stimulus of trade also affected scripts. As civilized communities expanded, merchants and traders often took over systems of writing and made them more efficient. Historians have noted that these changes, as well as the development of alphabets, occurred along ancient trade routes.

The speed and complexity of modern man's thoughts are certainly related to the developments in writing. One can imagine the ancient Egyptians or the people of the Indus Valley thinking at about the same pace as they were able to carve their hieroglyphs in stone or wood. Compare this to the speed that we can record our thoughts on an electric typewriter, or how rapidly Albert Einstein could communicate his ideas by means of letter and numeral symbols.

2

Deciphering Lost Languages

Go into any large library or museum where there are displays of ancient scripts, perhaps clay tablets stamped with Babylonian cuneiforms or papyrus manuscripts covered with Egyptian glyphs. You will probably wonder how anyone can make sense of these dead signs and fragments of languages that have never been heard by modern man. It is hard to imagine that there are living men who can read these puzzling records from the past as easily as we read books or newspapers in our own language.

How does one learn to read a language for which there is no dictionary, no grammar book or no clues as to how its words were sounded? How does one make any sense at all of a script in which all the vowels are left out, or of a writing in which all the letters or signs are run together so that there are no divisions between words? How does one read something in which the alternate lines are written upside down as shown here in the mysterious script of the Eastern Islanders?

People have always been intrigued by word puzzles such as acrostics, crossword puzzles, ciphers and rebus riddles. Solving rebuses became one of the most popular parlor games in Europe during the eighteenth century. Among such brain teasers, however, the decipherment of ancient scripts is the most fascinating because of the mysteries an unknown language might reveal and because of the intellectual challenge. The decipherer really starts from scratch; he has no dictionaries, grammers, code books or cipher keys to work with.

Actually the art of solving forgotten scripts is a young one. It had its beginnings during the Renaissance when Europeans became intensely interested in the ancient past, chiefly the arts, sciences and philosophies of classical Greece, Rome and the Holy Lands. It was further encouraged by the great explorations and discoveries made between the fifteenth and eighteenth centuries. But the real flowering of decipherments occurred in the nineteenth century as a result of a military campaign that failed. Napoleon Bonaparte's brief conquest of Egypt (1798–1801) focused the attention of Europeans on the enigmatic monuments and the curious hieroglyphic writing of the Pharaohs.

Although a few men had already tried to unscramble some of the mysterious scripts travelers had come upon in the Near East, it remained for the nineteenth-century adventurers and scholars to give the art of decipherment a true technology. They changed it from a haphazard study pursued by a few linguists and historians into a science. While first grappling with the unfamiliar writings

16

they encountered a number of problems we shall review here.

Imagine yourself faced with the task of cracking open a system of writing no living person has ever read or spoken. There are no textbooks to help you. Probably the first thing you will realize is that you must have enough examples of the script to work with because nothing can be deciphered from nothing.

Next, you must determine whether you are dealing with a known language written in an unknown script; for example, English written in wedge-shaped cuneiforms. Or is it an unknown language written in a known script, perhaps Sumerian written in Roman letters? Usually, if there are enough samples of such scripts, either combination might be easily solved. There is a third combination that is far more difficult, such as the Egyptian hieroglyphics in which the original language as well as the script were unknown.

Once you have decided which combination you are faced with, then you must figure out which way the writing runs. Not all languages, even those used today, are written and read from left to right; some go from top to bottom, some from right to left and, in another, one line is written from left to right and the following line from right to left. Egyptian hieroglyphics were normally read from right to left, yet hieroglyphics carved on monuments were sometimes read from left to right. Sometimes direction can be detected from the line endings. When we write or type a letter in English the right-hand margin is usually uneven, revealing which side of a page the lines begin. The direction an individual letter or sign faces can also offer clues. Most of the open letters in our Roman alphabet—E, F, G, K, etc.—face to the right. In Egyptian hieroglyphics many of the signs

face left, the normal reading direction.

Another preliminary task is to discover how words are separated from each other. In many ancient scripts the signs were run together without punctuation or spaces between words. Some clue might be worked out by keeping track of the repetition of the signs, the symbols or the letters. For example, if you run the words in the above sentence together—Somecluemightbeworke doutbykeepingtrackoftherepetitionofthesignsthesymbolsortheletters —note that one combination of letters (*the*) appears four times, suggesting it might be a common word and should be separated.

While you puzzle over word separations you should also be on the lookout for certain marks or strokes which appear more often than most signs. These are called word dividers, signs which the ancient scribes devised to show where words should be divided. In English we might as easily use a / instead of spaces—Some/ clue/might/be/worked/out etc.

Frequency counts, noting how often a word or sign is used, is one of the basic tools of modern code breaking, cryptanalysis and language decipherment. If you know a language thoroughly, especially some of the peculiarities of its structure, it can be of tremendous help in "breaking" one of the combinations where the language is known but the script is unknown. In English, for example, the letter *q* is always followed by *u*. In various languages certain letters occur more often than others. In English, *e*'s usually make up more than one tenth of all the letters used in a long composition. The next most used letters, are: *t, a, o, n, r, i, s, h, d, l*, etc. Different language systems have different peculiarities which might assist you, as a decipherer, in identifying them.

Some languages, both ancient and modern, use fewer vowels than others. Languages such as Egyptian and Hebrew used some vowels in actual speech, but in writing the vowel sounds were ignored and only consonants were written. A reader had to figure out which sounds were connected to the latter. Thus, if an Egyptian were to write *mstr*, it could mean *master, mister, muster, mystery.*

When you attempt to decode an unknown language you must also determine whether its script is alphabetic, syllabic, picto-ideograph, or a combination of these. The cuneiform writing of the forgotten Hittite civilization was a combination of ideograph word signs and syllabic signs. Again, frequency counts will reveal what the script is. Writing that makes use of fewer than thirty-five signs is usually alphabetic, each letter or sign representing a sound. Such scripts are often easiest to decipher. A writing system with fifty to a hundred signs will suggest that you are wrestling with a fairly complicated syllabary. A pictographic or picto-ideographic type of writing may have an endless number of signs.

By far the most useful clue a decipherer can hope to find is a bilingual or trilingual. These are passages or longer texts written in the unknown script and accompanied by parallel translations in some other language or script. Nowadays when governments make agreements or treaties the documents are written in the language and script of each party. So, also, in ancient times important edicts, laws and pronouncements were written in two or more languages, then engraved on stone tablets, pillars or temples. The most famous bilingual is the Rosetta Stone which contained the same carved message in three different scripts (two of them the same language, yet different forms of writing). Without the Greek text on the Rosetta Stone, it might have taken decipherers far longer to unravel the mysteries of Egyptian writing.

Even with the assistance of a parallel script in a known language, decoding a forgotten language and script is not always easy. If it is the script of an ancient empire, you search the parallel text (the known language) for proper names—kings, conquerors, priests, gods and geographic names. You try to find their equivalent in the unknown script. But sometimes this is no help. Names may be completely different in two different languages. By way of illustration, on Italian maps and in some English-language histories the Yugoslav seaport of Dubrovnik is called Ragusa.

In the absence of a bilingual you might try an etymological approach, that is, tracing and comparing the origin of words. Such a method was applied to some extent in solving the puzzling Minoan Linear B script and the Hittite language. But etymology can be dangerous, leading you on useless quests. The origin of similar-looking and -sounding words may be totally unrelated. Countless amateur anthropologists and a few noted scholars have fallen into this trap and have used like sounds or signs to prove that the Incas of Peru and the ancient Egyptians spoke the same tongue, or that the English and the Japanese must be related in some way because they both use the same-sounding word *so.*

You might, as have a number of notable decipherers, strike pay dirt by digging through the works of early writers and historians. Homer's tales of the Trojan War, believed by everyone to be legends, led to the discovery of the actual Troy and, later, to the solving of a Minoan-Mycenaean script. The Greek historian Herodotus, who traveled in the Near East more than four hundred years before the birth of Christ, provided clues instrumental in the "cracking" of Egyptian hieroglyphics, Persian cuneiforms and other forgotten scripts.

Some of the above are the problems you might face, and avenues you might explore, if you were to become a decipherer of forgotten languages. Today, of course, language code breakers are better equipped than their nineteenth-century mentors. If they are not experts, they are at least familiar with the work of philologists, linguists, language morphologists, archaeologists, historians, mythologists, mathematicians and other professional men and women.

In addition to being able to cope with some of the puzzles already mentioned, there is one other capacity a person should possess in order to be a successful decipherer. This is the ability to change direction quickly. Almost all decipherers at some time in their careers have made inspired guesses or worked with hunches that lead up a blind alley. Similarly, some men have had brilliant hunches which they abandoned because of the fury of their critics. You must sense which one might prove to be correct, which one may be a false lead. Sir Arthur Evans, who uncovered the fabulous Minoan civilization of Crete, spent years hoping to decipher the puzzling writing of this society, especially a script which he called "Linear B." He so firmly believed it was the written form of an unknown language that he made no progress at all. It took a young English architect, Michael Ventris, who was not a professional linguist, archaeologist or cryptanalysist, to crack the script. For a while Ventris believed the script was Etruscan, but his mind was flexible enough to abandon this false lead and toy with other possibilities. As a result, he solved one of the world's great puzzles.

3

The Mysterious East

Egyptian is not the oldest language in the world, nor did Egyptians invent writing, but any book about the quest and decipherment of lost scripts must necessarily begin with the cloudless land of the Pharaohs. Just as Columbus' voyage to the New World ushered in the age of discoveries, even though there were earlier intrepid seafarers, so too the solving of Egyptian hieroglyphics marked the beginning of the age of decipherments.

It seems strange that Egyptian writing should have been lost at all, because it has always been visible on tombs, monuments and obelisks. It is also remarkable that Europe lost track of Egypt's great civilization. For centuries the Western world had numerous ties with that part of the world. The Greeks traded with Egypt and built great cities on her shore; the Romans invaded Egypt, and Marc Antony fell in love with one of her queens. The region watered by the Nile was Rome's breadbasket. In later ages the Scriptures read by European Christians frequently mentioned Egypt and her kings.

Despite the numerous ties, Egypt was forgotten. The birth of Christianity in Roman times saw the beginning of the separation. By the reign of Emperor Justinian (A.D. 527–565) the Egyptian Christians, called *Copts*, separated from the Western Christian Church because they refused to recognize the divine nature of Christ. Freed from the domination of Rome, torn by centuries of internal strife and weakened by wars with Persia, Egypt was easily conquered by Caliph Omar's Moslem Arabs in A.D. 638. The break between East and West was complete. It was as if a wall of silence had been erected.

The few Christian pilgrims who sometimes reached Egypt during the Middle Ages wore blinders; they were only interested in Biblical history. If they noticed the pyramids, the Sphinx and other wonders, they regarded these as mysterious, inexplicable phenomena. And in Europe the Roman loot also seemed forgotten. No one noticed the statues of Ptolemaic kings carved when the Greeks dominated Egypt, or the Egyptian lions on the steps of the Roman capitol or the twelve obelisks scattered among the Roman plazas. Nor did anyone take an interest in the considerable fund of information about ancient Egypt that was buried in libraries and monasteries.

Most important of the ancient writers, whose works were stowed away in monastic libraries, was a Greek named Herodotus —the father of history. The son of a well-heeled family, Herodotus became the ancient world's most adventurous wanderer, but a drifter with a purpose. In 464 B.C., at the age of twenty, he set out on a seventeen-year trip, covering thousands of miles by boat, horseback and on foot. He visited the Aegean Isles, sailed the Black Sea to the estuary of Russia's Dnieper River, shuttled back across Asia Minor and Mesopotamia to the old Persian capital of Susa. He touched several African cities and completed a grand tour of Egypt. Wherever he went he interviewed people, observed their customs, took measurements and accumulated a rich store of information. All this he poured into a fat series of history books so beautifully written that Longinus, the Latin stylist, called them the "most Homeric of histories."

Herodotus was the first of the ancient writers to comment on hieroglyphic signs. He said: "On the pyramid of Cheops is shown an inscription in Egyptian characters giving how much was expended in radishes, onions and garlic for the workmen; which the interpreter, as I well remember, reading the inscription, told me amounted to 1600 talents of silver. And if this be really the case how much more was probably expended in iron tools, in bread, and in clothes for the laborers . . ."*

A handful of other writers also gave their impressions of Egypt. The Greek geographer Strabo and his contemporary Diodorus Siculus both traveled there shortly after the time of Christ; and we are indebted to Clement of Alexandria, the brilliant Christian theologian who was born in Egypt about A.D. 150, for the term *hieroglyphic*. In Greek the word means "engraved character." Perhaps the last of the ancient scholars to write about the Egyptian script was Horapollon, or Horus-Apollon who was born in Panopolis, Egypt, during the fourth century A.D. All these men, except Horodotus, lived at a time when hieroglyphic writing was past its golden age; the script was already four thousand years old and had changed in form.

The works of these early observers were almost as thoroughly forgotten as Egypt's civilization. Not until 1,875 years after the death of Herodotus were his *Histories* finally published in a Latin version. The first modern translation appeared in London in 1737. Strabo, too, was out of print for ages, the first modern translation of his works being published in 1805.

* Herodotus quotation from Book II, H. F. Cary translation.

Real interest in Egypt's ancient past was not aroused by such early writers. It was given impetus by a small number of adventurous travelers—English, German, French, Danish and Italian—who brought home exciting "I was there" stories about the Middle East.

One of the first of this daring company was Pietro della Valle, the handsome, dark-haired son of a noble Roman family. Pietro was a gay young man-about-town until, one day, his favorite girl married another man. He contemplated suicide. Fortunately, his closest friend convinced him that travel was the best cure for a broken heart. Thus from 1614 to 1629 he journeyed through Turkey, Mesopotamia, Persia, India and Egypt. He learned Turkish and Arabic. In Bagdad he married a native girl who shared his adventures, even taking part in a military campaign with Shah Abbas of Persia. After the death of his wife in 1621 he went to India, then to Egypt where he shaped the lively journal he had been keeping into a series of colorful letters which were published in Rome. On his return home he impressed Roman society with the large retinue of servants garbed in Oriental dress that followed him through the streets. He was received with great honors by Pope Urban VIII and was appointed "gentleman of the pope's bedchamber."

Not all visitors to the Near East were so handsomely honored. During the following century an inquisitive Scot, James Bruce, was fascinated by Egypt's Nile, the "mother of rivers." In June 1768, while visiting in Alexandria, he resolved to search for the sources of the Nile which he believed rose in Abyssinia. Since much of the region was controlled by Turkey he had sometimes to disguise himself as an Arab and at times as a Turkish sailor while making his way upriver. His adventures and narrow escapes from danger as he followed the Blue and the White Niles extended over five years.

When Bruce returned to Europe in 1773, Parisian scholars were intrigued by his descriptions and sketches of Egyptian monuments he had visited near Cairo, at Thebes and Aswan. However, in London, his reception was not as cordial. Newspapers, certain scholars who claimed to be Orientalists (a term applied to students of Near Eastern and Asiatic languages, history and antiquities), even some of his friends, ridiculed his accounts. They refused to believe him. As a result, he was unable to publish his lavishly illustrated five-volume *Travels to Discover the Source of the Nile* until 1790. How different it is today when men explore the craters of the moon!

French appetite was whetted by James Bruce's Egyptian adventures. France would soon send legions of brilliant investigators to probe the mysteries of Egypt. The French forerunner, Count Constantin François de Chasseboeuf Volney, was typical of so many of the eighteenth-century travelers. They were well educated, scholarly, keenly observant, adventurous and able to adapt to strange situations. Count Volney was well-to-do, a good writer, a politician and a philosopher of history. He spent four years in Egypt and Syria, and in 1787 he published a most perceptive book about his journeys there. He also spent time in prison and narrowly escaped losing his head by the guillotine. He served as a member of the scholarly French Institute, but also had the opportunity to snoop through the United States where he was arrested in 1797 and accused of being a spy.

During the eighteenth century almost everyone who did any serious touring was a spy. The great European powers were carving out empires in Asia, Africa and the Orient. France, England and smaller countries were dispatching diplomats, commercial agents, soldiers and scholars abroad in order to make surveys and alliances, and to stake out claims on huge hunks of African and Asian real estate.

The traveler-scholar-spy who did more to focus European attention on Egypt's forgotten writing, who, more than any other man, initiated modern Egyptology, was a self-educated farm lad named Carsten Niebuhr. He became the hero of an incredible saga, the sole survivor of a seven-year expedition across the razor-edged mountains and burning deserts of the Near East.

Niebuhr was born at Lüdingworth in Danish Holstein, not far from Hamburg, Germany, in the year 1733. The Niebuhrs were farmers, so Carsten passed his youth working hard in the fields and, when not needed for sowing, ploughing and harvesting, he received a country boy's schooling. When his father died, the family property, according to custom, went to the eldest son. Rather than stick around as a kind of hired hand, young Carsten set out for the German university town of Göttingen where he learned land surveying and math. He became an engineer in the Danish army, and at the age of twenty-seven he was invited to join an expedition sponsored by King Frederick V of Denmark. Its purpose was to explore Syria, Arabia and Egypt.

The expedition was an unusual one for its time. Before setting out, each member, including Niebuhr, spent an intensive year studying Arabic. Each man was also a specialist; the group included a surveyor, a philologist, a naturalist, an artist and a surgeon. In 1861 the men sailed for Alexandria. When they reached Cairo their movements were restricted for many months until Turkish travel permits were granted.

Niebuhr made good use of the long delay. Day after day, accompanied by the philologist Van Haven, he crisscrossed the region around Cairo surveying the Pharaonic monuments and temples. He became quite skilled at copying the puzzling hieroglyphic script engraved on them. This sort of occupation was not easy because the native Arabs and Turkish police were a constant annoyance, either throwing stones or threatening to arrest the two companions. Niebuhr was not easily discouraged. He sensed the importance of recording the strange writing so other scholars might have ample material to study. In his *Travels in Arabia and Other Countries* he wrote:

> To collect these scattered remains, would be a matter of great importance. Travelers seem to have neglected this care, or at least to have misemployed their pains upon it. They satisfy themselves with examining what can be seen for money, by paying an infidel guide. But they use no means to gain the friendship of the Arabs who rule in Upper Egypt. Without the good will of this jealous race, it must be impossible to make such research with ease or security. The Arabs, if cured of their natural distrust, would assist instead of obstruct the curious researches of strangers. But a person who would gain their friendship must stay longer in this country than is common . . .

Then he voiced a complaint that applies equally to many modern travelers. He said that too many travelers go to another country "merely that they may say they have been there." They learn nothing.

Young Carsten made a number of perceptive observations which, years later, proved to be helpful in the decipherment of hieroglyphics. He noticed in the carved signs: "Only the larger type are true symbols, the smaller ones seem merely to serve as explanation or to interpret the others." When Champollion eventually deciphered hieroglyphics, some of these small signs proved to be determinatives or signs that tell the category of the word. He also saw that the number of hieroglyphs was rather limited; there did not seem to be a sign for each individual word. He offered other clues when he wrote: "To facilitate the explanation of hieroglyphs, I have made out a table of such [glyphs] as occur more frequently in all inscriptions. It may be farther remarked that certain figures or characters occur often upon the obelisk and others again upon the fragments of tombs. This fact may be of some use in helping to an understanding of the meaning which they are intended to convey."

In the above comment Niebuhr had discovered, without realizing it, that Egyptians, like many other people, often used certain words and set formulas in writing edicts, grave inscriptions and dedications. Visit any graveyard and you may observe that we do the same, repeating such formulas as: "In Memoriam, here lies John Doe, beloved father of . . ."

The Danish expedition finally received travel clearance and set out for Mocha. Although most of its men were young, even they bent under the hardships of desert travel. The land was an inferno, the available food and water poisonous. Repeatedly, robbers and hostile natives troubled them. Van Haven and the naturalist Peter Forskål fell ill and died at Mocha. The remaining members of the party went on to Yemen, then set out for Bombay. On this leg of the journey the surgeon and the artist were both cut down and Niebuhr had to bury them. Thanks to a strong constitution, he survived attacks of both fever and dysentery.

Instead of returning home in dejection, Carsten Niebuhr single-handedly carried on the work of the expedition; he became its surveyor, naturalist, philologist and artist. To get around more easily, after leaving Bombay he adopted native dress; he lived and ate with the tribesmen he encountered. Burned as dark as a Berber warrior and speaking like an Arab, he journeyed alone to Shiraz, Persepolis, Muscat, Bagdad, Mosul and the ruins of Babylon. At the end of seven years of lonely, yet productive, wandering he returned to Europe. He paused in Paris to show his notes and sketches to French scholars, then settled in Copenhagen to write his vivid account of the long trek.

One sunny spring afternoon, thirty years after Carsten Niebuhr had visited in Paris, some of the same men he had seen were now gathered in the huge hall of the Institut de France to hear something more about Egypt. This time the speaker was a short, sallow-faced Corsican general, Napoleon Bonaparte. The general, his spectacular rise to fame just beginning, explained to the assembled scientists, artists and writers what their role would be in his planned invasion of Egypt. From time to time as he spoke, he tapped the leather-bound cover or flipped the pages of Niebuhr's *Travels in Arabia*. The book would be Napoleon's constant guide in Egypt.

Although Niebuhr's book inspired the Corsican, it in no way was responsible for the campaign in Egypt. The real cause was Napoleon's ambition to dominate Europe, an aim bitterly opposed by England. Napoleon felt he could deal a deathblow to England if he could occupy Egypt; he believed it was one of the keys to the world and an important route to India. He may have even imagined that by holding the land of the Pharaohs, he could threaten India.

Napoleon transported thirty-eight thousand troops across the Mediterranean, landing them at Alexandria on July 2, 1798. Following three weeks of scorching desert marches and a bloody battle with the armies of the Mameluke sultans, the French entered Cairo. Napoleon was able to stand upon one of the ancient pyramids at Gizeh and in a ringing voice tell his troops, "Soldiers, forty centuries are looking down upon you." But the glory of conquest was short-lived. On August 7, British warships under Adm. Lord Nelson cornered the smaller French Mediterranean fleet near Abukir and destroyed it. Napoleon's army was trapped in Egypt. The French adventure dragged on another year, but Napoleon's troops suffered from the debilitating heat, from hunger and from disease. On August 19, 1799, Napoleon abandoned his army and sailed for France.

The Alexander-like dream of the Corsican had failed as a military venture, but it did much for archaeology, linguistics and related studies. It marked the beginning of massive Egyptian studies because Napoleon's invaders included a curious contingent of men no army up to that time had even considered necessary. Napoleon took with him 175 intellectuals or savants, a kind of mobile think tank: engineers, linguists, surveyors, astronomers, Orientalists, poets and writers. They brought along crates of technical apparatus and a large library of books and pamphlets, everything that had been written about Egypt since the age of Herodotus. The French soldiers were amused by this novelty; they called these civilian experts "the donkeys."

Among Napoleon's "donkeys" there were two men who did as much to make Europe as conscious of Egypt and its forgotten civilization as Niebuhr had once done. One of these men was a talented gadabout, the other a serious scholar.

Baron Dominique Vivant Denon was certainly the most colorful of the two. He possessed a huge talent that had been quite visible in Europe long before he accompanied Napoleon across the Mediterranean. He was a lawyer, but at the age of twenty-three he turned to the theater and wrote a successful play, *Le Bon Père.* Then he switched to diplomacy and the arts, honing his skills as an etcher and illustrator while serving in the French embassies to Russia, Sweden and Switzerland. Although men relished his witty conversation (Voltaire was a close friend), women were especially charmed by him. He captivated Catherine the Great of Russia, Madame Pompadour, and later, Napoleon's Josephine. During the French Revolution he lost all his property and wealth; for a while he lived like a beggar until Jacques Louis

David, the great painter of the Revolution, introduced him to Josephine, who, in turn, presented him to Napoleon.

Although Denon had spent most of his life in the courts and embassies of Europe, in Egypt he became a new man. He fell in love with Egyptian antiquities. He out soldiered the French troops. They loved him and marveled how this fifty-one-year-old artist withstood the rigors of a military campaign in the desert. He often rode ahead of the troops in order to have more time to sketch, and frequently he was caught in the midst of a skirmish or battle.

The Cairo skyline enchanted him—the lovely mosques, the hundreds of minarets fingering the sky, the great dome of Jami-el-Ashar mosque. He spent days in the nearby desert marveling at the huge pyramids, gazing at the enigmatic expression of the great Sphinx of Gizeh, that half-man, half-lion that had crouched for ages in the desert.

Denon's artistic eye was particularly fascinated by the obelisks, those needlelike stone guardians of temple gates. He thought them beautifully proportioned and endlessly intriguing. At Thebes, while his soldier-companions were skirmishing with some straggling Mamelukes, and bullets whistled around his head, he sketched two impressive shafts. In his journal he described them thus:

> There were two obelisks of rose-colored granite, which are still seventy feet above the ground, and to judge the depth to which the figures seem to be covered, we may suppose about thirty feet more to be concealed from the eye, making in all one hundred feet for the height of these monuments. Their preservation is perfect, the hieroglyphics with which they are covered are cut deep, and in relief at the bottom, and show the bold hand of a master. What an admirable sharpness must the gravers possess, that could touch such hard materials! What time required for the labor!

Although Denon had no idea what the hieroglyphics said, he felt they were important. He copied thousands of the glyphs. He was able to note a difference in their styles. There seemed to be three techniques: some were cut in low relief, some were deeply engraved into the stone, others were hollowed out.

Denon shipped box after box filled with drawings to Paris. The sketches, notable for their precision of draftsmanship, caused a sensation. Denon, the gadabout, ex-lawyer, ex-diplomat, ex-lady's man, had become the first archaeological draftsman worthy of the name. Many of his etchings were included in his book *Voyage in Upper and Lower Egypt*, published in 1802.

Less colorful than Denon, but even more influential in bringing ancient Egypt to European attention, was scholarly François Jomard, one of Napoleon's chief "donkeys." Jomard, unlike some academic men who spend years in producing a slim dissertation, had a gargantuan capacity for work. In addition to supervising much of the research that was done in Egypt, he pulled together all of the work done by the French scholars, scientists and artists, fitting it in a well organized, monumental twenty-four-volume work titled *Description de l'Egypte*. Published between 1809 and 1813, it was an archaeological landmark.

Though Jomard's huge work contained a wealth of descriptions, countless drawings, copies of newly found papyrus texts, reports and surveys of ancient temples, and many of Denon's priceless etchings, a mystery remained. What was Egypt's story? Practically every etching of obelisks, columns, temples and monuments showed hieroglyphic writing—a profusion of signs, pictographs of animals, plants, mechanical apparatus, puzzling symbols. What did they say?

As Carsten Niebuhr had pointed out: "No people on earth were more anxious than they to transmit to posterity the memory of their revolutions, and of their knowledge, too, perhaps. No country in the world contains more inscriptions engraved on stones of the most durable nature, than Egypt . . ."

But no one, not a single man in the world, could read this writing. It was as if the Sphinx had created an insoluble riddle and had cast it into an impossible script. Even the natives of Egypt were mystified. They had not merely lost the ability to read the hieroglyphics, they had also forgotten who had built the monuments upon which the strange script was written. Dominique Vivant Denon told how, while he was sketching the monuments at Thebes, the headman of a nearby village asked him if it were not the French or the English who had erected the monuments and had written upon them.

4

It Is Scientifically Insoluble

Some years before Napoleon's invasion of Egypt a small number of inquisitive men tried to crack the Egyptian scripts even though the available examples of hieroglyphic were still limited. A half-dozen people, perhaps, came up with some interesting guesses, but no one made much headway because Horapollon's earlier theories about the glyphs had put them on the wrong track.

Horapollon, a Greek-Egyptian who had lived in the fourth century after Christ, had written a two-volume "study" of the hieroglyphics. This work, written in Coptic (a language descended from Egyptian, written in Greek characters and used by Egyptian Christians) was translated into Greek in the fifteenth century. From the Renaissance to the beginning of the nineteenth century Horapollon's *Hieroglyphica* was looked upon as the authoritative treatise because men believed the ancient glyph writing was still being used in Horapollon's time.

Horapollon believed that the hieroglyphs were symbolic pictograms and were not phonetic in any way. For example, he translated the pictogram of a goose as the sun. His reasoning for this was incredible. He said the sun produced warmth and a goose displayed more maternal affection (warmth) than any other animal or bird. It is hard to imagine how intelligent men could accept such reasoning and puzzle over Horapollon's long, nonsensical translations of the hieroglyphics.

The first man to come up with an important clue in deciphering the strange language was Athanasius Kircher, a German Jesuit priest, mathematician, inventor of the magic lantern and student of Coptic. In 1628, while rummaging through the library at Speyer, Germany, he uncovered an old book containing sharp engravings of an Egyptian obelisk which had been erected in Rome by Pope Sixtus V. Kircher spent more than twenty years trying to decipher the hieroglyphs of the obelisk as well as many others which he was able to track down. He wrote several books about Egypt and its script. His decipherments, however, made no more sense than those of Horapollon. Nevertheless he made one valuable suggestion; it was that Coptic, the dying language of the Egyptian Christians (which Arabic had displaced), was the popular language of Pharaonic Egypt. Two hundred years later a young Frenchman would prove him correct.

In the eighteenth century several Orientalists offered radical suggestions about the Egyptian writing, but generally they were laughed down because Horapollon's symbol interpretations were still popular. In 1740 the Bishop of Gloucester stated the hieroglyphs might not all be pictographs or ideographs, but that some might have phonetic values. At about the same time two French Orientalists, Abbé Jean Jacques Barthélemy and Joseph de Guignes, also stated that some of the signs might be phonetic. These men were supported by the noted Scandanavian linguist,

Georg Zoëga, who published, in 1797, a seven hundred-page survey of all the Egyptian material then known in Europe.

Zoëga not only felt the hieroglyphs might be phonetic, but he advanced another key clue to their decipherment. He thought that the cartouche 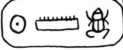 an oval encircling a group of signs—indicated names of royal personages. But Zoëga was also a pessimist because in his massive book he declared that the task of deciphering the Egyptian script was insurmountable. A little more than a decade later François Jomard thoroughly agreed with him. While in Egypt as a chief of Napoleon's brain trust, Jomard considered the hieroglyphs so untranslatable he discouraged even the copying and collection of them.

So little progress was made in decoding the ancient writing that the few correct clues which had been suggested by a handful of men were buried beneath an avalanche of wild theories about the ancient Egyptians and their language. Even reputable scholars indulged in incredible fantasies. One gray November evening in 1756 Joseph de Guignes, who had correctly suspected phonetic aspects, nevertheless rose before a meeting of the French Academy of Inscriptions and Belles-lettres and announced that the answer to the Egyptian puzzle would be found by studying Chinese characters; he had made a careful comparison of the two writing systems—obviously the Chinese were Egyptian colonists!

His sensational statement swiftly crossed the English Channel. Folks in London, where it had long been believed that the French always did things backward, vehemently disagreed with De Guignes. A few British experts argued that the Egyptians had originally come from China. Meanwhile in England and across Europe, Bible students were translating entire passages of the Psalms from the hieroglyphics. Other pseudoscholars claimed the glyphs were a secret code invented to hide astrological and Cabalistic messages.

Some down-to-earth scholars had already recognized that there were several forms of Egyptian writing and assigned different names to each one. They suspected that the hieroglyphic was the earliest Egyptian writing. As ages went by and writing materials changed, the hieroglyphics were abridged into a more easily written cursive form called hieratic script. The hieratic, in turn, was simplified, becoming the popular demotic script. Historians would eventually learn that the hieratic forms were used for all Egyptian literature until the demotic came into fashion, when hieratic was reserved for religious writing alone. Although serious scholars knew this, still they doubted that the script ever could be deciphered. The great Parisian Orientalist, Silvestre de Sacy, agreed with Jomard that the task was impossible. He said, "It is too complicated a problem; it is scientifically insoluble."

Carsten Niebuhr, the indomitable traveler, had had a cooler view of the problem. He wrote:

> As the relation between the allegorical figures and the ideas which they are employed to represent cannot be at all times equally evident; and as they depend often upon the way of thinking peculiar to those by whom the signs were invented, it is plain that writing of this sort cannot be legible without a key to explain the original signification of the characters. Some of the ancients have, indeed, explained a few of these symbols; but we meet with an infinite number of which nothing can be known. The hieroglyphs, therefore, cannot be deciphered because we want a proper key.
>
> Yet, I would willingly hope that the key to those mysterious writings of the ancient Egyptians may be yet recovered.

Approximately thirty years after Niebuhr penned these words, the "key" was found.

5

The Rosetta Stone

The key that unlocked hieroglyphic writing and opened the door to Egypt's tremendously long history was found in the Nile Delta, August 2, 1799.* At this time Napoleon's campaign was meeting reverses and French troops were erecting defense fortifications along the coast. Near the village of El Rashid (called Rosetta by the British) the ruined Fort Julien was being enlarged, and while working on this project, an Arab workman named Dhautpoul uncovered an oddly shaped stone. When its surface was cleaned, it appeared to be covered with strange writing. The native workmen were alarmed because they thought the writing was a dreaded magical incantation. They wanted to destroy the stone slab. Fortunately the attention of General Bouchard, the engineer in charge of the construction, was drawn to the stone.

The black basalt slab, now famed throughout the world as the

---

* There is some disagreement over the date when the Rosetta Stone was found. French historians give the August 2 date; E. A. Wallis Budge, a British Museum Egyptologist, says the stone was found late in July.

Rosetta Stone, was irregularly shaped, measuring three feet nine inches in height, two feet four inches in width. It was about eleven inches thick. On its polished surface were three broad bands of etched writing. General Bouchard saw that the upper band consisted of fourteen lines of hieroglyphics. The thirty-two-line middle band was unfamiliar; he thought it might be a Syrian script. The bottom band of fifty-four lines was in Greek. Parts of the stone were missing: the upper left- and right-hand corners as well as the lower right corner had been broken off so that some of the Egyptian and Greek lines were missing.

Bouchard sensed that the stone might be very valuable. If it contained the same message in three scripts, and one of them was in known Greek, could not the other scripts be deciphered? He immediately sent the stone to the National Institute maintained by French scholars in Cairo. Its importance was quickly confirmed. General Bouchard had erred slightly; the stone was not a trilingual, but a bilingual; the middle band was identified as a cursive form of hieroglyphic writing.

Napoleon himself came to look at the stone. He ordered skilled technicians to make lithograph-type copies and commissioned one of his generals to carry the prints back to France. These were sent to scholars in various parts of Europe. In Paris Professor Du Thiel, head of the National Institute, made the first translation of the Greek text. It proved to be a decree issued by the Egyptian priesthood at Memphis declaring their gratitude to the Greek ruler of Egypt, Ptolemy V Epiphanes, for gifts received: money, corn, endowments for the temples and remission of taxes. The decree was dated fourth Xandikos (March 27, 196 B.C.).

While experts in Europe puzzled over the copies, attempting to relate the hieroglyphic and cursive signs to the Greek text, the Rosetta Stone became a bone of contention. By 1801 the British had landed on Egyptian soil and had forced Gen. Jacques

François de Menou to surrender. According to the terms of capitulation the French not only had to give the British the conquered regions of Egypt, but they were required to hand over their invaluable collection of Egyptian antiquities.

A rich booty, indeed. During their campaign in Egypt the French had collected an enormous array of Pharaonic treasures: obelisks, statuary, sarcophagi, papyrus records and other material. All of this had been catalogued and copied by the "donkeys," then packed for shipment to Paris. Much of this loot was already stored in the house of General Menou in Alexandria. Although the French were willing to surrender most of their treasure, the Rosetta Stone seemed too important to give up. General Menou claimed it as his personal property and not liable to the terms of surrender. The British general, Lord Hutchinson, would have no such tricks played on him. He sent one of his officers to negotiate. This officer, Tomkyns Hilgrove Turner, was a professional soldier, an antiquarian and a diplomat. He visited with General Menou, exchanging cards and all the proper amenities, but to no avail. Monou and his aides refused to budge. Tempers flared. Someone in Menou's ménage vented his anger at the stone itself which had been carefully packed in a double matting of soft cotton and crated. The crate was opened and the stone dumped out. Recording this event, Turner wrote: "The covering of the stone was torn off, and it was thrown upon its face, and the excellent wooden cases were broken off. . . . When I mentioned the manner the stone had been treated to Lord Hutchinson, he gave me a detachment of artillerymen, and an artillery engine . . ."†

Off went Tomkyns Turner and his cannoneers. The show of force worked. Turner removed the Rosetta Stone to his own

† Turner's report on the taking of the Rosetta Stone was also printed in the British journal *Archaeologia*, Vol. XVI (London, 1812).

lodgings, then carried it to England aboard the frigate *l'Egyptienne*. In a speech before the Society of Antiquaries in London he described the odyssey of the stone and how it reached its present resting place in the British Museum: ". . . where I trust it will long remain, a most valuable relick of antiquity, the feeble but only yet discovered link of the Egyptian to the known languages, a proud trophy of the arms of Britain (I could almost say *spoila opima*), not plundered from defenseless inhabitants, but honorably acquired by the fortune of war."

By now scholars in every capital and university across Europe were brooding over copies of the Rosetta Stone. The Greek portion had been translated into a half-dozen modern languages. The other two scripts had been properly identified. It would appear, with this key at hand, that deciphering the hieroglyphics should be a snap. But no such luck. It took more than twenty years to unlock the Egyptian script. Although the French had lost their precious Rosetta Stone, the triumph of solving its secrets fell to a young Frenchman, Jean François Champollion.

The twenty years between discovery and decipherment were not wasted, of course. Several brilliant men fiddled with the Rosetta key, turning it this way and that way, but never enough. Two of these men, a Swedish diplomat and an English physican, made partial discoveries which eventually helped Champollion.

The first man to try deciphering the Egyptian texts on the Rosetta Stone was Silvestre de Sacy. Experts felt that if anyone could decode Egyptian it would be De Sacy. A brilliant Oriental scholar with an international reputation, he had deciphered and successfully explained Pehlevi, the Middle Persian language and script. He managed to spot in the cursive script of the Rosetta texts groups of signs that seemed to correspond to certain proper names in the Greek text—Ptolemy, Epiphanes and Alexandria—but this was as far as he went. The Stone stumped him.

De Sacy turned his notes over to David Åkerblad, a Swedish diplomat who had spent some years in the Near East. Åkerblad, at the time, was studying Coptic in Paris. He progressed where De Sacy had failed. He identified in the cursive (demotic) script all the proper names which occurred in the Greek portion, as well as the Egyptian words for "temples" and for "Greeks."

The Swedish diplomat did not go much beyond this because, like De Sacy, he believed that the demotic writing was alphabetical; actually, much of it was not. He also failed to note that Egyptian, like Hebrew, had no written vowels. But above all his work was hindered by De Sacy himself. When he showed his conclusions to the French scholar, the latter politely shook his head, saying, "You are running into a *cul de sac*—a blind alley."

Although Champollion was quietly achieving successes in France, by 1814 it looked as if an Englishman was on the verge of cracking the Egyptian scripts.

Sir Thomas Young, who came so close, was one of those remarkable Englishmen who, in their youth, give the impression that they might never amount to much. One of his Cambridge University classmates described him thus:

> His language was correct, his utterances rapid, and his sentences, though without affectation, never left an unfinished period, but his words were not those in familiar use, and the arrangement of his ideas seldom the same as those he conversed with. He was, therefore, worse calculated than any man I ever knew for the communication of knowledge.
>
> It was difficult to say how he employed himself; he read little, and though he had access to the college and university libraries, he was seldom seen in them. There were no books piled on his floor, no papers scattered on his table, and his room had all the appearance of belonging to an idle man.

Young was not idle, of course. He wrote and read Latin and Greek; he loved to solve puzzles; he was fascinated by calligraphy; he was as skilled at dancing on a tightrope as any circus performer. This was also the man who became a noted medical doctor as well as a physicist. The world of science remembers him as the discoverer of the main phenomena of vision and the laws related to the undulatory theories of light which laid the foundations of modern optics.

Young first saw the Rosetta Stone in the British Museum. Its puzzlelike nature challenged him, and he resolved to decipher it. He began working with a lithograph copy of the texts, as well as with copies of another important bilingual, the Greek and hieroglyphic inscriptions from an obelisk discovered along the Upper Nile in 1815 by Sir William John Bankes.‡

Since Young had no knowledge of Near Eastern languages he began his attack by making comparisons of the Greek and demotic texts. On sheets of parchment he pasted lines from the Egyptian script, and below each one a line from the Greek. He soon identified the demotic words for "Ptolemy" and "king," and several conjunctions which were frequently repeated.

David Åkerblad, now living in Rome, sent Young his own work notes, but these were of little use. Through his own com-

---

‡ Bankes was a noted traveler and companion of the poet Byron. In 1821 Bankes commissioned an unusual adventurer, Giovanni Battista Belzoni, to transport the twenty-six-foot Philae obelisk from the Upper Nile to London.

Belzoni's career as a transportation expert and amateur Egyptologist is worth mention. Belzoni was an Italian barber of enormous proportions (he was six feet eight inches tall). As a young man he served in various European armies, worked in a London circus as a strong man, then travelled through Spain to Egypt where he was employed as a collector of Egyptian antiquities by the British consul, Henry Salt. Belzoni's first major job was the transportation of the gigantic bust of Ramses II (called the Colossus

parative approach Young came up with some valuable discoveries. He saw a clear relationship between many of the signs in the demotic text and the hieroglyphic portion. He also deduced the meaning of certain glyphs though he did not know their sound values. By 1818 he had produced a hieroglyphic dictionary of 204 words, plus a list of 14 hieroglyphic phonetic signs. (Actually a quarter of his dictionary and 5 phonetic signs were correct.) Of great importance was his discovery that there were phonetic hieroglyphs among the purely ideographic signs.

He now tried deciphering the hieroglyphic text, beginning his attack upon the cartouche or oval which he believed enclosed the name of a king—Ptolemy.

The Ptolemy cartouche

of Memnon) from Thebes to the British Museum.

Shipping the Philae obelisk was an even more difficult task because the shaft was in one piece and weighed many tons. No dock was built to facilitate it being loaded on a riverboat, consequently the obelisk slipped from the boat. It took Belzoni days to fish it from the silty bottom of the river. There followed, then, the long trip downriver, navigating past the Nile cataracts.

In later years Belzoni operated on his own, plundering Egyptian temples and tombs in order to supply European museums. Although his archaeological methods were heavy-handed by today's standards, he is credited with discovering the tomb of Seti I, the father of Ramses II.

He took apart the signs and gave them phonetic values based on the Greek sounds for Ptolemy.

Thomas Young's phonetic values			*Corrected phonetic established later*
🔲	=	p	p
⌒	=	t	t
✗	=	(?) seems to mean zero or nothing	O (the letter)
🦁	=	ole	l
⬡	=	ma	m
44	=	i	y
⌐	=	os	s

Examining other cartouches, he worked out the name of Queen Berenice. His solutions were very close, though not perfect, be-

The Rosetta Stone, inscribed in Egyptian hieroglyphic (top) and demotic characters, and in Greek, with a decree in honor of Ptolemy V. It was discovered in 1799 at Rashid in the Nile Delta.

cause like De Sacy and Åkerblad he looked for vowels in the hieroglyphic script.

Young had gone about as far as he could. He had relied solely on his knowledge of Greek and his keen instinct for comparison and analogies. In 1817, writing to his close friend, Hudson Gurney, he said: "With the hieroglyphics I have done little or nothing since I last saw you—but I could never get to the end of them, as long as any materials exist unexamined and uncompared: I suppose they might furnish employment for an academy of forty members for a half century, and it will be enough for me to have discovered a mine by which others may enrich themselves . . ."

Why did Thomas Young yield the field to his youthful competitor, Champollion, whom he would soon meet in Paris? Perhaps he was satisfied, having given the key a partial turn. Perhaps he was anxious to get on with other experiments. Most likely, he realized he could not make much more progress with his system of comparisons, but needed greater knowledge of Near Eastern languages.

6

I've Got It! I've Got It!

Jean François Champollion was born in the village of Figeac,
Department of Lot, southern France. The circumstances surrounding his birth were so unusual that the villagers, today, still repeat
the stories with a sense of wonder.

During the summer of 1790, while Madame Champollion was
carrying the unborn genius, she became critically ill. When doctors gave up her case as hopeless her husband, Jacques Champollion, called in a witch doctor who lived in the nearby deserted
convent of Lundieu. The sorcerer, named Jacquou, applied his
secret remedies—herbs, balms and spiced wines. As if this were
not enough, he offered a prophecy. He said Madame Champollion
would give birth to a boy whose fame would be remembered as
long as there were famous men.

Needless to say, Madame Champollion not only regained her
health, but on December 23 she gave birth to an exceptional
boy-child. When the family physician, Doctor Janin, examined the

infant he was startled by its appearance: the child's skin was olive-tinted, the planes of his face were Oriental, and the corneas of his eyes were yellowish, a decidedly Levantine characteristic. It is said these markings became more striking when the child grew up; schoolmates and friends often called him the "Egyptian."

We do not know how much truth there is to these accounts, but we can be certain that young Champollion's early years were far from peaceful. Although the family was a closely knit one, political events often threatened it. In 1792 the French Revolution shook the country, and the following spring the Terror was unleashed. Jean François's older brother and his father were often involved in the political affairs.

Despite the turmoil the family managed to guide the boy into a career. Jean François was surrounded by books because his father was both a bookseller and an intellectual. The mother, reading Biblical stories to him from her missal, aroused his interest in Egypt and the Pharaohs. His brother, Jacques Joseph, who was twelve years older than Jean, further fanned this interest because for a while he had hoped to accompany Napoleon's "donkeys" to Egypt. A family friend, Father Dom Calmet, who had taken refuge in the Champollion home during the Terror, taught the boy Latin at a very early age.

When Jean François was enrolled in the village school, he appeared to be a rather poor student. He was indifferent to mathematics and sciences. Languages, however, appealed to him and he soon memorized long passages of Homer in Greek and Virgil in Latin. Brother Jacques Joseph somehow sensed, sooner than anyone else, that the boy had dormant talents of an unusual quality.

In 1801 the brother, now working in Grenoble, asked that ten-year-old Jean François be sent to him so that he could attend a better school than those in Figeac. This marked the beginning of a remarkable relationship between the two brothers. Although the older brother would soon become a well-known archaeologist, he was so convinced that young Jean François would do more for the family name than he could, he began calling himself Champollion-Figeac and, later, simply Figeac. In turn, to show his indebtedness, Jean began calling himself Champollion the Younger.

The period in Grenoble was an exciting one for young Champollion. Grenoble, a beautiful city set against a sparkling backdrop of the snow-clad Alps, was the intellectual capital of the Dauphiné region. Champollion attended an excellent school run by Abbé Dussert where he began an intensive study of Hebrew. Within a year he stunned the school inspectors during an oral exam by giving a penetrating translation and interpretation of the Old Testament in the original text. Shortly after this he impressed another visitor, Jean Baptiste Fourier. Fourier, a noted mathematician and physicist, had served as one of the chiefs of Napoleon's scientific commission in Egypt and had written the introduction for Jomard's monumental *Description de l'Egypte.*

Intrigued by young Champollion, Fourier invited the dark-skinned boy and his older brother to his home to view his valuable collection of Egyptian antiquities. The visit, in the fall of 1802, was a turning point in Jean François' life. He was enchanted by the Egyptian artifacts, but especially by the rich array of hieroglyphic inscriptions on stone tablets and papyrus rolls.

"Can these be read?" Champollion asked excitedly.

Fourier shook his head. "No one has been able to, as yet."

Cheeks flushed with ardor, the boy said, "I shall read them. Not yet, but in a few years I shall."

Fourier was amused by the lad's enthusiasm, but he was also impressed by his intelligent questions. He invited young Champollion and his brother to attend evening gatherings held regularly at his home. These meetings firmly set the boy upon his career—the conquest of Egypt's enigmatic written language.

But Champollion was not yet ready to tackle the hieroglyphics. His own innate good sense, plus the mature guidance of his brother and Fourier, convinced him that he must properly prepare for the task. He must learn everything he could about Egypt. He must learn the languages of the Near East. He must study philology and calligraphy. His enthusiasm for knowledge burned like an intense flame. At age thirteen he began studying three more languages—Arabic, Chaldean and Syriac. In the room he shared with his brother he covered the walls with hieroglyphic signs; since he could not read them, he read about Egypt in the pages of Herodotus, Strabo, De Guignes and Abbé Barthélemy.

When he was sixteen he began his first major Egyptian project, a chart and chronology of Egypt under the Pharaohs. During the summer of 1807 he submitted the outline to the lyceum of the Grenoble Academy, the most learned institution in the city. On September 1 he read his paper before an audience of professors who expected to hear nothing more than a callow schoolboy's paper. When he had finished there was a moment's silence, then applause; President Renauldon of the Academy embraced him, and the gathered professors immediately agreed to elect the slender youth to their faculty.

His mentor, Champollion-Figeac, who was now working in Paris, felt it was time for the precocious young scholar to study in the capital.

The Paris interlude, lasting a little more than a year, was both rewarding and depressing. The capital offered Champollion the best teachers. He studied Persian, Sanskrit, Arabic and Coptic, learning them so rapidly and well that they made him feel even more Oriental. He wrote of himself: "Arabic has completely changed my voice; it has grown soft and throaty. I speak almost without moving my lips and this must heighten my oriental appearance for yesterday Ibn Saoua mistook me for an Arab, salaamed when I spoke in his tongue."

Among all these languages Coptic most enchanted him, and within a year he spoke and wrote it so easily that he kept his diary in that language. "I am in fact a Copt," he wrote, "who for his amusement translates into that language everything that comes into his head; I speak Coptic to myself so that no one will understand me."

His moods in Paris swung like a pendulum from emotional highs to bitter lows. The high points included the opportunity of seeing and studying in the Louvre an excellent plaster-of-Paris copy of the Rosetta Stone which had been cast in Cairo before the original stone was surrendered to the British, and equally exciting, a meeting with Silvestre de Sacy.

The accounts of this meeting, written by biographers, vary considerably. Some say that the famous, middle-aged Orientalist was suspicious of the teen-age student because the latter seemed too cocky; others picture Champollion as being unusually shy and the older man being deeply impressed by him. We do know with certainty, at least, that De Sacy discouraged Champollion from attempting to decipher Egyptian scripts, telling him it was a waste of time, that he would not possibly succeed.

The most depressing periods in Champollion's stay in Paris were caused by his financial situation. In addition to pursuing his studies, he had hoped to get a job and earn enough money so he could marry a hometown girl. He found no job. Instead he had to rely on his brother for what little assistance he could give. He had to live in a cold, eighteen-franc garret room near the Louvre. He had so little money that he scarcely ate; his clothes were worn to threads, and he was often sick. In later years he recalled this period with irony, saying, "Archaeology is a beautiful girl without a dowry."

Forced to abandon his studies in Paris, he returned to Grenoble in 1809 to occupy the Chair of History at the Lyceum. He was eighteen; a professor teaching his former schoolmates. On August 7 of that year he presented to the Academy the first results of his Egyptian studies. It was a startling paper for in it he advanced the radical idea that the three forms of Egyptian writing were related and, in order to understand the hieroglyphics found on early monuments, decipherment must begin with the later demotic forms. He may not have realized it at the time, but he had spied the path leading toward a solution of the Egyptian riddle. He had done it four years before Thomas Young began dabbling with the glyphs.

Although Champollion was a dedicated scholar, he was not one of those men who ignores the world around him. Like countless Frenchmen, he held passionate political views. He believed in the Republic and opposed Napoleon's dictatorship. He wrote satires, essays and political songs ridiculing the self-made emperor. And he suffered as a consequence of his fervor and outspoken nature. Older professors and politicians resented his brilliance, and for a while he was deprived of a fourth of his academic pay. "My lot is decided," he complained. "I must be as poor as Diogenes. I must buy myself a barrel to live in, and sacking to wear on my back." When Napoleon was overthrown in 1814 Champollion bitterly wondered if the new regime was any better.

Shuttling back and forth between politics and scholarship, he continued working on a Coptic dictionary which he felt would help him in the attack on the Egyptian scripts. The book kept growing and growing. When he had reached page 1,069, he wrote his brother: "My Coptic dictionary is getting thicker day by day.

The author, meanwhile, is getting thinner."

On March 1, 1815, Napoleon escaped from exile at Elba, returning to France for one hundred dramatic days. On March 7, the Corsican entered Grenoble. Here he interviewed Champollion-Figeac, who became one of his secretaries. The general also met Champollion the Younger. Even though Jean François was not an enthusiastic supporter of Napoleon, the two men conversed at length, mostly about Egypt and Champollion's Coptic dictionary. With an imperial gesture, the would-be emperor promised to have it published.

But Napoleon's days, even as a sponsor of a Coptic dictionary, were numbered. After his defeat at Waterloo and his banishment to St. Helena, the Bourbon kings returned to power.

In Grenoble both Champollion and his older brother became involved in an unsuccessful revolt opposing the return of the Bourbons. The brothers barely escaped arrest; for months they hid in the Dauphiné Alps. Young Champollion's teaching post at the lyceum was abolished. By the end of the year the pressure let up somewhat, but during the next six years Champollion was never certain what the next day would bring: at times treason charges were raised against him, at times he was allowed to teach.

During this time he returned to his first love—the Egyptian riddle. In 1821, while another treason charge haunted him, he worked feverishly with the hieroglyphic and hieratic signs from the Egyptian *Books of the Dead*,* the texts of which had been

* The *Books of the Dead* were papyrus rolls containing ritual prayers, poems and illustrations that were buried with the dead. These were supposed to assist the spirit of the dead in a safe passage to afterlife. Many of them contained what has been called "negative confessions of sins," that is, "I have not murdered; I have not sinned in the temple; I have not done evil to men; I have not ill treated animals," etc.

published in Jomard's twenty-four-volume work. By fall he accomplished something no one else had ever done: he transliterated a demotic text, sign by sign, into hieratic script, then transposed this into hieroglyphics. He now had proof of the evolution of Egyptian writing.

Demotic version of the name Ptolemy

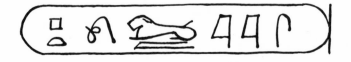

On his thirty-first birthday, December 23, 1821, he had a brilliant idea. It was so simple one wonders why no one else had thought of it. He decided to make a total of all the signs in the Egyptian texts of the Rosetta Stone, as well as a total of all the words in the Greek. text. The Egyptian signs appeared 1,419 times. In the Greek there were only 486 words. This suggested to Champollion that each glyph or sign did not represent a whole word, as was generally believed; there were too many of them. He felt that combinations of the signs made words just as combinations of our alphabetic letters form words. Thus, many of the glyphs must be phonetic signs.

During the following month he began transliterating all the demotic signs from the Rosetta, especially the Greek names which provided him with phonetic keys. Working with names enclosed in the oval cartouches (now assumed to be royal names), he noted that there was only one oval-enclosed name on the Rosetta Stone, but it was repeated six times. Its simplest form was this:

But it also appeared as this:

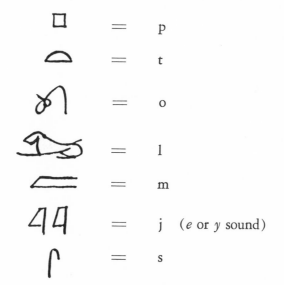

The longer version of the Ptolemy cartouche on the Rosetta Stone

Sir Thomas Young had already deciphered it—the name of Ptolemy, one of a dynasty of Greek (Macedonian) kings who ruled over Egypt. Like Young, Champollion broke the word down to its sound equivalents, but with his keener knowledge of Near Eastern languages he avoided Young's mistake of fitting vowels into the script. His work notes looked like this:

□   =   p

△   =   t

=   o

=   l

=   m

=   j   (*e* or *y* sound)

=   s

Champollion's phonetic values for the Ptolemy signs

Thomas Young's alphabetic spelling of the name was *Ptole-maios*; Champollion's transliteration was *Ptolmjs*, the *j* represent-ing an *e* or *y* sound. But now the young decipherer needed proof that the signs in the cartouche really represented Ptolemy, and that these same letters could be applied to a different name con-taining similar or almost similar letters. This proof arrived during January 1822. Champollion received lithograph copies of the bi-lingual inscriptions from the Philae obelisk. He immediately spotted the glyphs for *Ptolmjs* in the Egyptian text, and it was confirmed by the Greek text.

But something else electrified him—a different name in a royal cartouche! According to the Greek script it was Cleopatra, wife and sister of one of the Ptolemys. When he compared the signs in the two ovals it was obvious how some of them matched:

The Cleopatra cartouche from the Philae obelisk

Constructing a new line from the Cleopatra oval, he filled in the signs with the letters he already knew:

C   L   E   O   P   A   T   R   A

Cleopatra's name. Sound values similar to Ptolemy signs are underlined.

He had observed that sometimes the ⬡ sign was replaced by the ⬭ glyph, so he considered them homophones, both standing for *t*. Thus he was left with two vulture signs, a mouth-shaped sign, a right-angle triangle sign and the odd terminal or tenth sign—all still unknowns. Champollion knew that in the Greek spelling of Kleopatra, as in our language, there are two *a*'s. He decided the two vultures represented *a*. Since he had determined the value of most of the signs it was natural to imagine the △ glyph stood for the Greek *K* sound. Thomas Young and others had already noticed that the terminal sign ⬡ always followed the name of a queen, princess or goddess; it stood for no sound. The only sign left without a phonetic value was the ⬭ glyph; simple logic impelled Champollion to believe it represented an *r* sound. Thus, Kleopatra was deciphered. From these two names he derived eleven signs which corresponded to eleven consonants, vowels or dipthongs in the Greek alphabet.

In some of the cartouches additional signs followed the name of Ptolemy. A careful reading of the Greek text on the Rosetta Stone showed Champollion that these were royal titles meaning, "Ever-living, beloved of Ptah." His knowledge of Coptic phonetics helped him determine their sounds and add several more signs to his list. Now, almost like the image on photographic paper responding to the developing solution in a darkroom, familiar names began to appear among Champollion's many samples of hieroglyphics—names out of the past: Alexander, Antonius, Tiberius, Germanicus.

Champollion-Figeac and several friends wanted the young man to reveal his findings. Champollion was not ready to broadcast his hieroglyphic discoveries, but on August 22, 1822, he nervously read a treatise on the demotic script before the Paris Academy. When he had finished, he was startled by the acclamation; men who disliked him, men who had discouraged him, suddenly hailed him. The great De Sacy rose and stretched out his two hands to the young scholar, proposing that the government publish the treatise.

A visitor in Paris, Sir Thomas Young, met Champollion at the Academy. He was impressed, yet wondered if the Frenchman was going too fast. He wrote to his friend, Gurney:

> And Champollion has been working still harder upon the Egyptian characters. He devotes his whole time to the pursuit and he has been wonderfully successful in some of the documents that he has obtained—but he appears to me to go too fast—and he makes up his mind in many cases where I should think it safer to doubt. But it is better than to do nothing at all, and others may separate the wheat from the chaff when his harvest is complete. How far he will acknowledge everything which he has either borrowed or might have borrowed from me, I am not quite confident . . ."

Champollion was more cautious than Young had imagined. Despite the progress he had made, the young man from Figeac was not sure how far his phonetic keys to Egyptian would work.

Since he had been struggling with texts from the Ptolemaic and Roman periods, he had not yet found a true Egyptian name. For a while he feared that only foreign names and titles were written phonetically. Nevertheless, a month after reading his treatise before the Academy, the real breakthrough occurred.

On the morning of September 14, he opened a new collection of inscriptions, finding among them copies of a script taken from a rock temple at Abu Simbel on the Nile. The temple had been constructed long before the Greeks and Romans occupied Egypt.

He gave a sudden start when he noticed the first oval cartouche. Obviously it contained the name of a king, but it was unlike any of the late Egyptian period names he had been reading so often.

Cartouche with name of Rameses in hieroglyphic

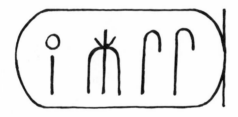

He recognized the last two signs—shepherd crooks, which stood for *ss*. Then what? His brain seemed to hesitate, then mesh swiftly as though working with a rebuslike puzzle. He knew that the first sign, a circle, was a pictograph for the sun. Circuits in his brain clicking. In Coptic the word for sun was pronounced "Rē." Did the first and last signs in the oval represent *Rē-?-ss*? He remembered running across the three-pronged middle sign on the Rosetta Stone hieroglyphics; the Greek text translated this sign as "to be born" or "birthday." Again, in Coptic the word for "birthday" or "give birth" was pronounced "mise." Just shorten it to *m* and slip it in between the *Rē* and the *ss. Rē-m-ss!* Was it possible? Could this be Ramses, one of the most famous of ancient Pharaohs?

Then he found another cartouche that made his brain spin.

Name of the Pharaoh Thutmosis or Thotmes

He jumped at the first sign, a pictograph of the ibis, the sacred bird of the god Thoth. It was followed by the three-pronged glyph and the shepherd staff. Reading the signs phonetically they seemed to say *Thot-m-s*. Champollion sat there in a daze, pronouncing the name over and over: "Thotms, Thotmes, Thutmosis . . ." Thothmes, indeed, another name famous among the ancient Egyptian dynasties.

There was no longer any doubt in the mind of the decipherer. The phonetic system was clear. He had turned the key and opened the door to a history that had been lost for fifteen hundred years.

But Champollion had learned caution and thoroughness. Though he had made the breakthrough in the early morning, he spent hours checking and rechecking his material. By midday he was satisfied. He gathered his notes and examples together and set out to tell his brother. He hurried through the streets of Paris, bumping into pedestrians, not aware that they were there, because his mind was in Egypt. He arrived at the Institute where his brother worked and hurried through the library to Figeac's reading table. He threw his papers upon it, crying out in hoarse elation, *Je tiens l'affaire!* ("I've got it!"). Then he collapsed upon the desk.

He had so exhausted himself that he was bedridden for a week. At times he imagined he was dying. He pleaded deliriously, "My God, give me another two years, just two more years." At last, after regaining his strength, he wrote a résumé of his discovery to Bon-Joseph Dacier, president of the French Academy of Inscriptions and Belles Lettres. On September 29, at the request of Dacier, he read his landmark résumé, *Lettre à M. Dacier relative à l'alphabet des hiéroglyphes phonétiques,* before a full gathering of the Academy.

In his address Champollion credited the many people who had helped him. He told the audience, "Scholastic criticism is indebted first to the talents of your illustrious colleagues M. Silvestre de Sacy, and successively to the late M. Åkerblad and Dr. Thomas Young for the first accurate ideas drawn from this [Rosetta Stone] monument."

The members of the Academy gave him a tremendous accolade, but the finest tribute came from Thomas Young who said, "If he did borrow an English key, the lock was so dreadfully rusty, that no common arm would have had the strength enough to turn it."

News of Champollion's achievement spread rapidly across Europe. Many scholars, of course, were dubious, some attacked him bitterly because his work was not entirely free of errors. The controversy raged until 1866 when the great Egyptologist, Richard Lepsius, soundly confirmed Champollion's decipherments.

In the hundred years since Champollion's discovery, tremendous advances have been made in recovering Egyptian history. The language and scripts have been re-created, full grammars and dictionaries have been compiled. These after-efforts have not always been easy; scholars still encounter blind spots because the development of Egyptian writing and literature had extended over five thousand years. The signs, their meanings, the ways of pronouncing them changed from age to age. The idiom of Egyptians who lived around 3000 B.C., for example, was no longer easily understood by Middle Kingdom Egyptians a thousand years later, while Middle Kingdom idioms became almost incomprehensible to their descendants about 1500 B.C. When the Macedonian dynasties held sway over the ancient land, then Roman and Christian influences followed, the language and script went through still greater changes.

Although controversies over his discoveries continued during his lifetime, Champollion ignored them. His health, affected by years of privation, bouts of diabetes and tuberculosis, had deteriorated. He felt he was going to die, but he continued to work feverishly, fully using the few years left to him.

From 1824 to 1826 he traveled in Italy, copying and cataloging papyri collections at the Vatican Library, in Florence and in Turin. From a garret in the Turin Academy he wrote to his brother about the twelfth-century B.C. Egyptian list of kings he had found: "I was spellbound. In front of me was a table, ten feet long, covered in its entire breadth with a layer at least a half-foot deep of paypri fragments. I was able to savor dates of which history had lost all recollection, and the names of gods who had had no altars in more than fifteen centuries."

In 1828 a lifetime dream came true. He was given the opportunity of leading an expedition to Egypt. It was like returning home to a land he had never lived in. Afterward he returned to

Paris and, despite poor health, taught Egyptology at the Collège de France until the early months of 1832. Suddenly, at the age of forty-two he became critically ill. He complained, "Too soon, too soon—there is so much inside my head." He died on March 4, 1832. Although the government ignored his funeral, many of Europe's men of science attended his burial at Père Lachaise cemetery in Paris. Silvestre de Sacy, Bon Joseph Dacier and Baron Alexander von Humboldt were among his pallbearers.

7

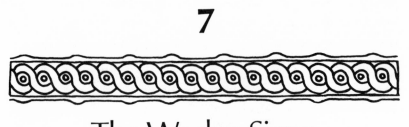

The Wedge Signs

At about the same time that Egyptian hieroglyphics had begun to fascinate European scholars, travelers in the Near East were uncovering another mysterious script, the wedge-shaped cuneiform signs which had been completely lost for a thousand years.

Descriptions of this system of writing were extremely scarce. A few early historians—Diodorus, Athenaeus and Eusebius—mentioned it when speaking of Assyria and Babylonia. Herodotus, in his fourth book, described two columns which had been erected at the edge of the Straits of Bosphorus, the gateway between Europe and Asia Minor. The columns had been placed there by order of King Darius I of Persia who had died the year before Herodotus was born. Both shafts bore bilingual inscriptions in Greek letters and the curious wedgelike signs which Herodotus called *grammata Assyria* ("Assyrian characters"). Unfortunately, none of these early historians gave information about the nature of the wedgescript.

It is amazing that cuneiform writing was forgotten by men both in Europe and the Near East. For centuries it was one of the great systems of written communication, holding together empires that stretched from the shores of Greece to distant Persia. Like our Roman alphabet, cuneiform signs were the vehicle for numerous languages: the Sumerians who spoke an Indo-European tongue used it; the Akkadian (Semitic speaking) people of Babylonia and Assyria wrote in cuneiform; other forgotten civilizations—Elamite, Mede, Hittite, Hurrian and Urartaeans—recorded their own languages in it.

The cradle of this ancient method of writing was the Mesopotamian region, the once fertile plain sandwiched between the Tigris and Euphrates rivers. Today it is called Iraq. Though much of the area now appears bleak and dusty, it was in Mesopotamia where man first seemed to domesticate plants and grain. Here various cultures piled one upon another over a period of five thousand years. Exotic cities rose and fell—Nineveh, Babylon, the older, forgotten Ur.

Cuneiform writing had no Horapollon to whet and misguide European interest. The first modern mention of it occurred about the middle of the seventeenth century, the information coming from Persia rather than Mesopotamia. About this time Persia was ruled by the Safavi Dynasty, shahs noted for their friendliness toward European visitors. Leading the list of travelers was the Portuguese ambassador to the Persian court, Antonio de Gouvea. He was followed by John Cartwright, an Oxford student, by Sir Thomas Herbert, and by Frenchmen and Spaniards.

Most of these men visited Persepolis, the capital built by Darius I and Xerxes between 500 and 464 B.C. In their journals they described the cuneiform inscriptions such as those at Takht-i-Jenshid, but these early travelers were puzzled and unable to identify the script. Spaniard García de Silva Figueroa said: "The signs are triangular, but extend like a pyramid or a small obelisk so that they are all indistinguishable from each other except by their direction and arrangement."

What these observers did not know was that the form of the signs was related to the original writing materials. The ancients used a stylus with a triangular end which they pressed into soft clay. In appearance the writing looked like bird tracks left in wet mud. The clay tablets were baked hard and stored in the equivalent of libraries. The writing was also carved on stone monuments in the same wedge pattern. Unlike Egyptian writing, which gradually changed from the hieroglyphic signs to the smooth-flowing hieratic and demotic scripts, cuneiform signs, during their thousands of years of use, hardly changed the basic wedge characteristics. As different cultures took them over they were simplified and fewer wedges were used.

The first person to bring back actual cuneiform inscriptions was Pietro della Valle (mentioned in Chapter 3). The flamboyant young wanderer brought a few baked cuneiform tablets from Babylon and sketches of inscriptions he had seen at Persepolis. In his published letters he suggested that each cuneiform sign represented an idea or word. He tabulated the frequency of certain signs and came to conclusions which were of no earthly assistance to later decipherers. He could not read the script, of course.

Cuneiform signs brought to Europe by Pietro della Valle

⟨ 𝖸 𝖳𝖳𝖳 𝖸 ⟨▷⟨⟨ 𝖸𝖸

A more important traveler and collector of cuneiform inscriptions was Jean Chardin, son of an affluent Parisian jeweler. In 1666, when he was twenty-one years old, he set out for the Near

East on a diamond-buying trip. In the course of his eleven years in the East he traveled through Turkey, Armenia and Mesopotamia, finally settling in Isfahan, the new capital of Persia, where he became purveyor to the Shah's court. His adventures in Persia were as colorful as those in the *Arabian Nights*, but more important to us is that he was the first European to carefully study the cuneiform inscriptions at Persepolis and nearby Naqsh-e-Rustam. He copied a trilingual inscription (in Elamite, Old Persian and Akkadian-Babylonian, which no one could read or identify) that would spur European interest in deciphering the strange writings. He also vigorously opposed the current belief that cuneiforms were mere decorations.

When Chardin returned to Paris in 1677, French persecution of Huguenot Protestants forced him to flee to England where he was well received. In London he was knighted and appointed court jeweler by Charles II. He served the English court in various capacities, but devoted most of his latter years to Oriental studies. Though spurned by his own countrymen, he was buried with honors in Westminster Abbey. The story of his Persian journeys, *Travels of Sir John Chardin*, still makes lively reading.

In 1714, a year after the publication of Chardin's *Travels*, the mystifying wedge-shaped signs finally received the name that has stuck—cuneiform—from the Latin *litterae cuneatae* ("wedge or nail letter"). Engelbert Kämpfer, who coined the term, was another of those nomad-scholars who contributed to the recovery of this ancient writing. Although he was educated for the ministry (his father was a Westphalian pastor), he wandered off to study in various European capitals until he was proficient in medicine, physics and natural sciences. Joining a Persia-bound exploration party financed by King Charles XI of Sweden, he traveled through Mesopotamia and widely in Persia.

During a three-day visit at Persepolis he said, "To copy the sculpture and inscriptions of all these buildings would take more than two months." By forgoing food and rest those few days he managed to take numerous measurements and copy one important inscription. He did not realize that this inscription would be one of the keys to the decipherment of Babylonian cuneiforms.

All these men performed useful, though limited, functions in the rediscovery of cuneiform writing, but it remained for Carsten Niebuhr, who had helped focus attention on Egyptian hieroglyphics, to supply European scholars with enough material to make possible the decipherment of one of the cuneiform scripts—the Old Persian.

During March 1675, Niebuhr spent more than three weeks at Persepolis, surveying the ruins and making the first accurate copies of the carved inscriptions. He was quick to realize that some of them were not uniformly written but seemed to be three separate scripts. Perhaps these were a trilingual? Three different languages? On the basis of one of these scripts he made remarkable deductions. He decided that the signs should be read from left to right; he concluded that some of the signs might be alphabetic, and he established an alphabet of forty-two signs. Thirty-two of these have been proven correct, an unusual accomplishment for a man who had accompanied the ill-fated Danish expedition simply as its surveyor.

We might imagine, since trilinguals had been found by Niebuhr and others, that the cuneiform decipherments might proceed rapidly. In truth, the task was more challenging than decoding the Egyptian hieroglyphics. The trigraphic Rosetta Stone and the bilingual Philae obelisk provided the decipherer with at least one known language. The inscriptions found in Persian sites were in unknown languages and an unknown script. Resolving them was like trying to work out an algebraic problem with three unknowns.

De Sacy, had he been asked, might have gloomily replied, "It is too complicated a problem; it is scientifically insoluble." Nevertheless, Orientalists and linguists in England, France, Germany and other countries began nibbling at the puzzle. Since most of the cuneiform inscriptions these men studied had come from Persia, it seemed logical that one of the wedge scripts might be related to the Old Persian of the Achaemenian Dynasty (sixth to fourth centuries B.C.). But the Persian tongue, ancient or middle, was no longer a living language. It had long ago been replaced by Greek, Parthian and Arabic.

But again, as with Champollion's beloved Coptic, a religious sect seemed to have preserved fragments of Persian. Throughout the country's long, turbulent history the followers of the prophet Zoroaster (Zarathustra) had preserved Old Persian writing in the Zend-Avesta scriptures. They guarded their knowledge in the years after Alexander the Great's conquest, about 330 B.C., and throughout the later Parthian and Sassanian domination, but following the Arab conquests and the supression of Persian scripts after A.D. 638, they fled to northern India. Their descendants, called Parsees, retained their identity and Zoroastrian traditions. Obviously, someone had to go to the Parsee teachers, the *dasturs*, to find traces of Old Persian.

A young Frenchman, Abraham Hyacinthe Anquetil-Duperron, took on this task. While studying for the priesthood he became so fascinated by Near Eastern languages that he abandoned his religious calling. In 1755, at the age of twenty-three, he received a small study-grant from the government and free passage to India. He wandered over India for seven years, learning Sanskrit and modern Persian. He spent much time in the Parsee settlements north of Bombay where he studied with the holy men and prepared a translation of the Zend-Avesta.

On his return to Paris in the spring of 1762, he began readying his translation for publication. He made his notes, his translation and the 180 rare Oriental manuscripts that he had brought back from India available to Silvestre de Sacy, the towering figure in Oriental studies. The material made possible De Sacy's successful decipherment of Pehlevi or Middle Persian.

Following the publication of his Zend-Avesta translation in 1771, Anquetil-Duperron retired from public life. Demoralized by the French Revolution, he withdrew from society and, like the Parsee holy men he had known in India, he lived in voluntary poverty, finally dying in Paris in 1805. Although he never tried deciphering the cuneiforms, his quest of the Zoroastrian scriptures contributed to the eventual recovery of Old Persian because, among other things, he revealed forms in Old Persian of historical names that were only known in Europe in distorted Greek forms.

Meanwhile other amateurs and scholars continued gnawing at the problem, each clarifying some point. In 1798, Oluf Gerhard Tychsen, a librarian at Rostock, Germany, and specialist in Arabic and Hebrew, while working with Niebuhr's Persepolis copies, noticed the constant repetition of a curious wedge-shaped sign. He determined it was a word separator placed at the beginning and end of words to divide them from each other.

At about the same time Christian Earl Münter, the Danish Bishop of Seeland, also discovered the word separators. He went even further. In analyzing the Persepolis cuneiforms he determined that the limited number of signs in one of the trilinguals indicated it must be alphabetic, that the second text must be syllabic, and the third text was made up largely of ideograms. He also believed the Persepolis scripts dated back to the period of Persia's great kings, Darius and Cyrus, rather than to the Parthians who ruled some three hundred years later.

The intelligent bishop also drove the first small wedge of decipherment into the mysterious wedge-shaped cuneiforms. He saw that a certain group of signs were frequently repeated in one of the texts. Relying on his knowledge of titles in Middle Persian, he made a shrewd guess.

"King" in Old Persian cuneiforms

He believed the signs stood for "king." He also felt that the word before the title would be the name of the king. He was quite right about the title, but he was never able to decipher the names of the kings.

8

To Win a Wager

Often in the history of great discoveries people not trained in a specific science or profession have leaped the fence to make an important find in a seemingly unfamiliar field. Hiram Bingham, a college professor of Spanish colonial history, scrambled up the cloud-shrouded peaks of Peru and found Machu Picchu, a "lost" Inca city, the existence of which most qualified archaeologists doubted. Benjamin Franklin, a printer, discovered certain properties of electricity. The same curiosity, the same spark of genius causing these men to stray into another discipline or profession, also affected Georg Friedrich Grotefend, a humble schoolteacher who first pried open the cuneiform script, clearing the way for the solution of ancient Persian writing.

Grotefend was born in Münden, Germany, June 9, 1775. His father was a shoemaker of limited education and means, but he seemed ready to scrimp and sacrifice so that the boy might better himself. Although Georg exhibited a talent for languages, his aims in life were modest. He did not want to be a great scientist, philosopher or statesman. He was satisfied to become a good schoolteacher and, if the opportunity arose, to become a school principal.

He worked hard in the lower schools and went on to the Paedagogium, a teacher's prepatory at Ilfeld College. He was then hired as an assistant instructor in the municipal lower school at Göttingen. Here there were more opportunities for self-advancement, for Göttingen had one of the best universities in Germany. In his spare time Grotefend attended university lectures in theology, philosophy and the new science of philology. After a few years he was appointed to a permanent teaching post in the Gymnasium, a secondary school preparing students for university.

He had reached what appeared to be a comfortable rut. He performed his daily teaching chores. He enjoyed spending an occasional evening in a *bierstube* drinking with colleagues and friends. He dabbled in two harmless hobbies: he wrote minor papers about old European languages, and he solved puzzles. His friends were amused by his passionate interest in acrostics, word games, rebus puzzles, conundrums and riddles. Sometimes they were amazed by the vast store of collateral information—classical history, Biblical lore and other data—he had accumulated in his mind in order to solve riddles.

One evening while drinking with friends, according to some Grotefend biographers, one of his pals challenged him to solve an insoluble riddle. The friend bet him that he could not decipher the cuneiform scripts. Although he was not a boastful man, twenty-seven-year-old Georg Grotefend agreed to the wager, saying, "I can do it."

The story may or may not be true, but we know that Grotefend had already become interested in the enigmatic writing; he had read some of the works of De Sacy, Kämpfer and Tychsen. Although he was not a professional Orientalist, nor had he any ambition to become one, he had a knack for languages and a penchant for puzzles. Somehow he got copies of Niebuhr's Persepolis inscriptions and began studying the cuneiforms. His rich store of historical information came into play immediately, and his logic was admirable.

He assumed that the cuneiform texts were in three different languages, and that all three were about the same topic because in the ancient world important edicts were usually translated into more than one language. Since the inscriptions had been found in an early Persian site, and because it was common practice to place the most important language text in the middle, he felt that the center column was written in Old Persian.

His next deduction was again based on history. Agreeing with Bishop Münter's theory that the inscriptions dated from the period of the Achaemenian kings, he decided that one of the other scripts in the trilingual must be Babylonian. Drawing upon his knowledge of Herodotus and other Greek historians, he knew that Cyrus the Great, founder of the Old Persian kingdom, had conquered the Babylonians in 540 B.C. Normally a victor publishes edicts in his own language as well as in the language of the vanquished.

Like a dog worrying a bone before finally cracking it, Grotefend continued nibbling here and there before attempting a decipherment. He reviewed the theories of his predecessors. With one, he agreed that the cuneiform lines should be read from left to right; with another, he agreed that one of the trilingual texts was alphabetic, a second was syllabic and the third mostly ideographs. Then he came upon Bishop Münter's "king" signs, and a sudden spark danced through his memory.

He recalled Silvestre de Sacy's decipherments of Pehlevi or Middle Persian. De Sacy had discovered that the Sassanian king at Naqsh-e-Rustam was always referred to in a kind of formula:

"Z——, great king, the king of kings, the king of Iran and non-Iran, the son of Y——, the great king." De Sacy mentioned this type of inscription was traditional among the Persians. Grotefend asked himself, "If this form was traditional, why shouldn't it have been used by Persian kings living at a much earlier period?" A logical question: we moderns use forms of address which have been traditional for hundreds of years. We announce a queen, saying, "Her royal highness, Queen of England, Wales and Scotland," or we address a prelate as "His Eminence, Cardinal X——, archbishop of Y——."

The young German schoolmaster turned his attention to the Niebuhr-Persepolis inscriptions and scrutinized the middle text.

He went over the signs hundreds of times; then, all at once, he noticed several distinctive features. The "king" signs in the first section are repeated as words number 2, 4 and 6; in the second sections as words number 2, 4 and 7. For illustrative purposes we have placed parentheses around each of these words. The frequently repeated signs $\wedge$ are the word separators discovered by Oluf Tychsen. Grotefend also noted that the "king" signs, with several added signs attached to them, appeared in word number 5 in both sections. He decided they might be the genitive or possessive plural, meaning "of kings."

He saw something else that puzzled him: the first word in section one and word number 6 in section two contained the same signs, but in section two the additional signs ⟨▷⟨ had been inserted in the middle. Words number 1 and 6 are shown in parentheses, the insert in brackets. His knowledge of Middle Persian suggested that these inserts might be another genitive form meaning "son of." He felt, furthermore, that the first word in each of the above sections might be a royal name.

Working at first with section one, he made the following translation, substituting letters for the unknown words: X——, great

Old Persian cuneiforms decoded by Grotefend

Section One   (Darius)

Section Two   (Xerxes)

king, king of kings, king of A———, son of Y———, the ?———.

The puzzle-solving schoolteacher became excited. He had the makings of a sentence, a sentence out of cuneiforms, but it was a riddle sentence still unsolved. It seemed to him that the key was in the names represented by X and Y. His rich stock of classical lore again proved invaluable. He dug into his Herodotus and, in the seventh book, the Greek historian has Xerxes speaking to his uncle, Artabanus: "For I should not be sprung from Darius, son of Hystaspes, son of Arsames, son of Ariaramnes, son of Teispes, son of Cyrus, son of Cambyses, son of Achaemenes . . ."

The lines spoken by Xerxes suggested a dynastic succession: So-and-so, the son of So-and-so, who was the son of So-and-so. But which names to choose from this treasury of historical names? Going back to the cuneiform texts, he spied a subtle difference between the two texts. In the first one "great king" was linked to X———, and "son of Y" seemed not to be a king.

In the second inscription which he had translated as: "X———, the great king, the king of kings, the son of king Z———, the ?———," the final Z——— was linked to a king. It suddenly dawned on him that he must find a line of ancient Persian rulers in which the son and father were kings, but the grandfather was not. Remembering that the Achaemenians ruled over Persepolis, he felt the two kings he was searching for must be from that dynasty. He found them by a system of elimination:

> I began to check through the royal successions to determine which names most neatly fitted the inscriptional characters. I decided they could not be Cyrus and Cambyses because the two names in the text did not begin with the same initials, nor could they be Cyrus and Artaxerxes because the first appeared too short and

the second too long. There were no other names left but Darius and Xerxes, and they fitted so easily that I had no doubt about making the right choice. This agreement was secured because in the son's inscription the father's name had the royal sign beside it, whereas this sign was lacking in the father's inscription.

Hystaspes, of course, was never given the title of king by Herodotus and other early historians. Thus Grotefend was able to fill in the unknowns. Transcribed into English, the two decipherments read:

(Section One)

Darius, great king, the king of kings, the king of countries, the son of Hystaspes, the Achaemenian . . ."

(Section Two)

Xerxes, great king, the king of kings, the son of King Darius, the Achaemenian . . ."

Although he was elated, Grotefend was not satisfied. He had been using the Greek form of the names; now he wanted their Old Persian equivalents in order to establish the sound values of each cuneiform sign. His familiarity with the Hebrew pronunciation of some of these names, and relating these to pronunciations furnished by Anquetil-Duperron's translation of the Zend-Avesta, enabled him to work out sound values for thirteen cuneiform signs.

On September 4, 1802, Georg Friedrich Grotefend stood before the Göttingen Academy and presented his solution. Hardly anyone in the audience seemed aware that the simple schoolmaster had performed a brilliant feat. In less than a year he had cracked the Old Persian cuneiforms, doing it with very little material and without the assistance of any text in a known language.

Instead of hailing his discovery, the academic authorities at Göttingen refused to publish his treatise because he was not a professional Orientalist. They shook their heads; he was too young, a mere twenty-seven-year-old schoolteacher. Ninety years would pass before Göttingen University got around to honoring this genius by publishing his full text. Nevertheless, a few men saw its value. Silvestre de Sacy wrote a full account of Grotefend's decipherment in a French journal, *Magasin Encyclopédique.* Oluf Tychsen also published excerpts from the treatise. For the most part, however, Orientalists simply ignored it.

In Paris there existed another key to Old Persian cuneiforms which, if anyone could have read it, would have supported Grotefend's discovery. It was an engraved copy of inscriptions from an alabaster vase that had belonged to King Xerxes. This copy had been published by Count Caylus in 1762. Its text was in four languages—Old Persian, Elamite, Babylonian and Egyptian. Grotefend had to wait until Champollion deciphered the hieroglyphics in 1822 before the Caylus text could confirm his own decipherment.

Although Grotefend continued tinkering with cuneiforms until his death in 1853, he remained an unknown, unhailed explorer of languages. Perhaps the stresses of daily schoolteaching and administration (he became the principal of a grammar school in Frankfurt am Main and director of the Gymnasium at Hannover) prevented him from going much beyond his original cuneiform solution. He lived long enough, however, to watch another man completely solve the cuneiform scripts, not merely Old Persian but the Akkadian wedges hiding the rich treasure house of Assyrian-Babylonian history.

9

Rawlinson and
the Behistun Rock

When Grotefend worked with the inscriptions from Persepolis, he began the unraveling of the middle text—Old Persian (Achaemenian). For many years the identity of the remaining two texts was a mystery. Now we know, of course, that these other languages were Elamite and Akkadian (Babylonian-Assyrian). Before telling the story of how they were identified and decoded, let us take a quick look into the history and the movements of the people of the Near East, especially Mesopotamia and Persia. It will reveal why so many languages were written in cuneiform and why two-, three- and four-language inscriptions were carved on monuments.

The first kingdoms or city-states to rise in the Mesopotamia region were the communities of the Sumerians, builders of the cities called Lagash, Ur and Kish which were located in the south where the Tigris and Euphrates rivers join and flow into the Persian Gulf. From about 3000 B.C., they shared the rich region with the Semitic Akkadians who had come from the Syrian desert. Gradually their culture was absorbed by the Akkadian-Babylonians. About 2400 B.C., the Amorite nomads swept into the region from the Syrian desert, fusing with the Akkadians to create a great Babylonian Empire. Still later another Semitic people, the Assyrians, who had prospered along the northern reaches of the Tigris, began to dominate the entire region. From about 1300 to 600 B.C., they created an empire that ruled over most of the Near East—Mesopotamia, Syria, Palestine, Phoenicia, much of Persia and Egypt. The Assyrian-Babylonians were in turn conquered by the desert Aramaeans and the Chaldeans.

Meanwhile, in southwest Persia (Iran) a non-Semitic people called the Elamites had developed their own civilization and maintained cultural and commercial contacts with their Sumerian-Babylonian-Assyrian neighbors. During the first millennium B.C., a people who called themselves the Arya or Aryans began moving from the great steppes between the Black Sea and Caspian Sea into the cultivated lands of Iran. The Arya included some ten to twelve tribes, the Medes and Persians among them. Some of these adopted the language and writing of the Elamites. Cyrus, the king of Anshan in Elam, the founder of the powerful Achaemenian Dynasty, used this language.

Beginning with Cyrus, the Persians created an enormous empire stretching from northern India to the Mediterranean, including Mesopotamia and, for a while, Egypt. Later the entire region was conquered by the Greeks under Alexander the Great, still later by the Romans, then by the Arabs.

Although this historical review has been considerably simplified, we should keep in mind the fact that during this long stretch of time there were constant military struggles, cities rising and falling, people moving from one area to another. We should remem-

The "Darius, King of Kings" inscription at Ganj-i-Nameh near Kirmanshah. It served as one of the keys used by Henry Creswicke Rawlinson in deciphering ancient Persian cuneiforms.
PHOTO: COL. WALLACE D. BARR

ber that the wedge-shaped cuneiform script was invented early in this period and was adapted for different languages as new kingdoms or empires appeared. Thus, for example, sometime between 555 and 529 B.C., during the reign of Darius I, the Persians abandoned Elamite, which Cyrus had used; they developed their own language and cuneiform script. But because they ruled over the Elamite country, over Mesopotamia and their own land, they wrote important inscriptions in Old Persian, Akkadian-Babylonian and Elamite.

One would imagine that once Grotefend had found the key to the Persian cuneiforms the full translation of the Persian texts would move along swiftly, and these would serve as a key to the Babylonian and Elamite texts. No such thing occurred. A number of important Orientalists and linguists applied themselves to the problem. Over a span of several decades they identified a few more cuneiform signs, they translated another nineteen historical names, and they increased the number of Old Persian signs with known phonetic values to thirty. All in all progress was snaillike.

Then the big breakthrough came. It was made by Henry Creswicke Rawlinson, an English soldier who originally had had no intention of becoming an Orientalist. Rawlinson was, again, one of those unusual men who could leap the fence into another field and succeed spectacularly.

Rawlinson was born at Chadlington, Oxfordshire, on April 11, 1810. His family was comfortably situated, but not wealthy. The best education they could provide was at Ealing School where he learned Latin and Greek, read the classics, and distinguished himself as an athlete. Since his family could not afford to send him to university, he took the path that most ambitious young men choose at that time—a career in India. He secured a commission as a cadet in the military service of the East India Company.

At the age of sixteen he began the long sea voyage around Cape Horn. While aboard ship he made the acquaintance of an elderly, notable passenger, Sir John Malcolm, governor of Bombay. The latter was a scholarly man, and during their frequent conversations he kindled Henry's interest in the history and language of Persia to such an extent that, while fulfilling his duties as a subaltern this first year in Bombay, young Rawlinson began to learn Persian, Arabic and Hindustani. He picked up languages so rapidly that at the end of the year he was made interpreter and paymaster of the First Grenadier Regiment.

Although he was a passionate student of Persian literature and memorized long passages from the Persian poets, he was no intellectual drudge. He was gay and convivial, making friends with almost everyone. He enjoyed gambling and took great delight in winning wagers. He was an excellent horseman, and as one of his fellow officers remarked, "Rawlinson could outride, out shoot and outwit all of us." Naturally promotions came quickly; when he was hardly twenty-three, his administrative abilities were so appreciated he earned a promotion to major.

In 1833 Rawlinson reached the land of his dreams—Persia. He was sent there with several fellow officers to reorganize the Shah of Tehran's troops. While enroute he made a detour in order to visit the ruined palace of Darius the Great at Persepolis where he was fascinated by the cuneiform inscriptions. A year later, having accomplished his mission at Tehran, he was sent to Kirmanshah in Iranian Kurdistan to serve as military adviser to the Shah's brother, the provincial governor. And again he made a detour in order to copy some trilingual cuneiform inscriptions carved on the slopes of Mount Elvend, just south of Hamadan.

Settling down at Kirmanshah, in this remote corner of Iran, Rawlinson tried his hand at deciphering the Elvend trilingual. At this time he was totally unaware that Eugène Burnouf, a noted Orientalist in Paris, was also puzzling over copies of the same inscription; nor did he know anything about Grotefend's early decipherment of the first lines of the Persepolis inscriptions. His approach was similar to Grotefend's, but he was even better equipped for this kind of puzzle solving than the German school-master. The young major spoke and read modern Persian with ease; he knew several dialects, especially the Bakhtiara dialect which bore some similarities to Old Persian; and he was extremely well read in ancient history.

Within a very short time he determined that one of the Mount Elvend texts had been written for King Darius, son of Hystaspes; a second had been written for King Xerxes, son of King Darius. He deciphered these names as well as four others. Here in Kurdistan, far from the scholarly academies and libraries of Europe, he had, on his own, gone beyond Grotefend.

In Kirmanshah, the governor and his followers greatly admired the young Englishman. He was a good military adviser. He could recite the great poets. He rode like a native warrior. They were fascinated by his interest in the ancient writings. Anxious to help him, they told him about some huge inscriptions and carved reliefs on a mountain wall less than twenty-two miles away. It was called Behistun ("place of the gods") a mountain with twin peaks dominating the plain of Kirmanshah, guarding the ancient caravan road that wound from Hamadan, former capital of the Medes, to distant Babylon.

During the summer of 1835 Rawlinson made his first trip to Behistun. He was stunned by what he saw. On the sheer southern face of the mountain, he made out an imposing memorial cut into a great beam of stone. He thought it stood 160 feet or more above the valley floor. It was so high its details were hardly visible. The major dismounted and focused his spyglass upon what he guessed was a victory monument hewn upon the sheer rock wall.

He made out two figures standing to the left, carved in bold relief and seemingly poised in the shimmering air. They appeared to be court dignitaries. To their right stood a larger royal personage whose right hand was raised toward a winged sun while his left hand held a Persian bow. One foot of this kingly figure rested upon the head of a prostrate man. Behind the man, and facing the king, were nine prisoners, feet bound, ropes tied to their necks. What did the strange scene depict? Rawlinson's companions, members of the governor's staff, had no idea at all.

Within a year he would be able to tell them. The imposing monument had been carved to celebrate the deeds of Darius, King of Persians, to memorialize his victory over a group of rebellious princes. The royal figure represented Darius; the prostrate figure was that of Gaumata, a priest who had encouraged the nine princes in their rebellion. The great panel had been carved in 516 B.C.

Rawlinson wondered why this huge memorial had not come to the attention of scholars. It had stood for centuries within view of an ancient trade route. "Each year," he wrote of it, "pilgrims from the east climb these sacred heights, and descend to Najaf, Kasimein, Kerbela and Mecca." Actually, other Europeans had seen it. A Greek physican, Ctesias, had visited Behistun in the fourth century B.C. The Latin writers, Diodorus and Siculus, mentioned the rock's cuneiform inscriptions. In 1807 a French emissary to Tehran thought the bold relief figures were of Christ and his twelve apostles.

Although the sculpted figures were impressive, Rawlinson was far more intrigued by the fourteen columns of cuneiform script

A GREAT GOD IS AHURAMAZDA, WHO
CREATED THIS EARTH, WHO CREATED
YONDER SKY, WHO CREATED MAN, WHO
CREATED HAPPINESS FOR MAN WHO
MADE DARIUS KING, ONE KING OF
MANY, ONE LORD OF MANY. I AM
DARIUS THE GREAT KING, KING OF
KINGS KING OF COUNTRIES
CONTAINIG MANY MEN, KING IN
THIS GREAT EARTH FAR AND
WIDE, SON OF HYSTASPES AND,
ACHAEMENIAN, A PERSIAN,
SON OF A PERSIAN, AN ARYAN,
HAVING ARYAN LINEAGE.

خدای بزرگ اهورامزدا است، که بزرگترین خدایان
است، که این زمین را آفرید که آن آسمان را آفرید که مردم را خلق
فرمود که مردم شادی داد که داریوش را پادشاه نمود یگانه شاه
از میان شاهان بسیار و یگانه فرمانروا از میان فرمانروایان
بسیار من هستم و داریوش شاه بزرگ شاه شاهان شاه کشورهایی
که ملتهای بسیار دارد شاه این سرزمین بزرگ دور و دراز
پسر ویشتاسب پهناور

Sign beneath the Ganji-i-Nameh cuneiform inscription containing
both English and modern Iranian translations of the Darius
memorial. PHOTO: COL. WALLACE D. BARR

which had been cut into the rock beneath these figures. The arrangement of the panels of script suggested that it was a trilingual. But what a trilingual! It was longer by far than all similar inscriptions found anywhere; it was longer than all of them combined. He immediately grasped their importance. The texts might be filled with proper names and place names. The messages seemed long enough for someone to work out the grammar and vocabulary of the forgotten languages.

During the summer and fall Rawlinson frequently visited Behistun; the twenty-two miles was a mere early morning jaunt for a horseman like himself. On each trip he tried to copy a part of the Old Persian text, since he knew it would be the easiest to decipher. The job was not easy. Even though he used a spyglass, the shimmering heat, the glare of the sun, the swirling dust made it impossible to accurately read the signs. At last, he decided the only way to do it right was to climb the sheer face of the wall.

Two biographers of Rawlinson describe this feat, reporting that the youthful major let himself down from above with ropes, then swung back and forth like a pendulum while copying the cuneiforms. Rawlinson, in his own journal, understates the danger somewhat. Instead of swinging down from ropes, he said that he climbed to the recess where the Persian script began. He did this several times a day without difficulty, simply by extending a plank over gaps he could not leap. Then, in his words:

> On reaching the recess which contains the Persian text, ladders are indispensable in order to examine the upper portion of the tablet; and even with ladders there is considerable risk, for the footledge is so narrow, about eighteen inches or at the most two feet in breadth, that with a ladder long enough to reach the sculpture sufficient slope cannot be given to enable a person to ascend, and, if the ladder be shortened in order to increase the

slope, the uppermost inscription can only be copied by standing on the topmost step of the ladder, with no other support than steadying the body against the rock with the left arm, while the left hand holds the notebook, and the right hand is employed with the pencil. In this position I copied all the upper inscription, and the interest of the occupation entirely did away with any sense of danger.

To reach the Elamite version of the text, Rawlinson ran into greater danger because he had to extend a ladder horizontally to bridge a chasm with a sheer drop of more than a hundred feet. On his first try the ladder came apart; he was left hanging over the chasm, desperately clinging to what remained of the ladder. He could hear part of the ladder crashing upon the rocks far below:

> . . . assisted by my friends, who were anxiously watching the trial, I regained the Persian recess, and did not again attempt to cross until I had made a bridge of comparative stability. Ultimately I took the cast of the Sythian [Elamite] writing by laying one long ladder, in the first instance, horizontally across the chasm, and by then placing another ladder, which rested on this bridge, perpendicularly against the rock.

While residing in Kirmanshah and frequently galloping out to Behistun, Rawlinson made handsome progress in deciphering the Persian script. By early 1837 he had translated nearly two hundred lines of the Achaemenian text. On his return to Bagdad the same year, he received from the British Resident Agent there copies of the cuneiform studies being done in Europe. He must have experienced a thrill of elation after looking at these reports because he had already established more phonetic values and meanings for the Old Persian signs than all the other scholars combined.

The Behistun Rock.

Toward the end of 1837 he sent reports of his work to the Royal Asiatic Society in London. Its secretary-director, Edwin Norris, sent a copy to Eugène Burnouf of the Société Asiatique in Paris. Burnouf and his colleagues were so impressed they elected Rawlinson an honorary member of their organization.

In 1839 the work Rawlinson was doing on the cuneiforms was interrupted for some five years. Civil war had been brewing in Afghanistan. The twenty-nine-year-old major was dispatched to Kandahar where he organized, trained and commanded a unit of Persian cavalry. The rumblings of revolt finally exploded. On May 29, 1842, when Kandahar was threatened by insurgent troops, Rawlinson led his horsemen into battle and won a brilliant victory. His superiors were so impressed by his abilities that they offered him a promotion and attractive opportunities for advancement. Although a fine career as a military leader lay before him, he had become more interested in scholarship. At the end of the year he resigned his commission and returned to Bagdad where he replaced Colonel Taylor as the British Resident.

A new, equally colorful period of life began. Although he had abandoned soldiering, Rawlinson ran the Residency as though it were the headquarters of an Eastern potentate. He organized a company of Sepoy guards to patrol the estate. When he went out or came home, drums were beaten and arms were presented. He always wore a gorgeously braided officer's cap, and in Bagdad, amused friends claimed that if Rawlinson were to put the cap on his dog and sent the dog out on an errand, everyone in the streets would step out of its way and soldiers would present arms.

The Residency became the gathering place for illustrious visitors. Rawlinson, a connoisseur of Indian and Persian food, put on elaborate dinners. On such occasions, after dessert, cheese and cigars had been served in the drawing room, the gentlemen were invited to return to the dining room where the table had been cleared and a great tureen of hot punch was set out. Then, while deviled herring, turkey legs and other snacks were passed around, toast after toast was drunk. Austen Henry Layard, the excavator of Nineveh, and a frequent visitor at the Residency, complained that after such evenings he felt quite queasy the next morning.

During this time Rawlinson frequently returned to Behistun. He was a stickler for detail. He wanted his copies of the Darius inscription to be absolutely accurate. He had begun making paper impressions or casts of the cuneiform texts. By 1847 he had made a copy of the Babylonian version which was harder to get at than either the Old Persian or Elamite scripts. Since he was too large framed to squeeze his way up to the carvings, he enlisted the aid of a human mountain goat. He described the project thus:

> I found it quite beyond my powers of climbing to reach the spot where it was engraved, and the cragsmen of the place, who were accustomed to track the mountain goats over the entire face of the mountain, declared the particular block inscribed with the Babylonian legend to be unapproachable. At length, however, a wild Kurdish boy, who had come from some distance volunteered to make the attempt . . .
>
> The mass of rock in question is scarped, and it projects some feet over the Scythic [Elamite] recess, so it cannot be approached by any of the ordinary means of climbing. The boy's first move was to squeeze himself up a cleft in the rock a short distance to the left of the projecting mass. When he had ascended some distance above it, he drove a wooden peg firmly into the cleft, fastened a rope to this, and then endeavored to swing himself across to another cleft, at some distance on the other side; but in this he failed owing to the projection of the rock. It then only remained for him to cross over to the cleft by hanging on with his toes and fingers to

the slight inequalities on the bare face of the precipice, and in this he succeeded, passing over a distance of twenty feet of almost smooth perpendicular rock in a manner which appeared quite miraculous. When he had reached the second cleft the real difficulties were over. He had brought a rope with him attached to the first peg, and now, driving in a second, he was enabled to swing himself right over the projecting mass of rock. Here with a short ladder he formed a swinging seat, like a painter's cradle, and fixed upon this seat, he took under my direction the paper cast of the Babylonian translation of Darius . . .

Having deciphered the Old Persian script, Rawlinson turned his attention to the the more difficult Elamite and Babylonian cuneiforms. One can imagine how trying it must have been, working in the oppressive heat of Bagdad. In order to concentrate, Rawlinson invented an unusual kind of air conditioner. In the exotic garden of the Residency he set up a waterwheel which dumped buckets of water upon the tin roof of a kiosk. He sat at a table beneath this open pavilion, quite able to work while the dripping water reduced the heat from a scorching 120 degrees to a comfortable 95 degrees. As he puzzled over the cuneiforms his favorite pet, a lion cub which had been found in the rushes of the Tigris River, dawdled beneath his chair.

After spending considerable time with the Elamite text, Rawlinson came to the conclusion that it was not quite as important as the Babylonian version. He had discovered it was a syllabary; it might take endless time to work it out. He now turned to the Babylonian cuneiforms, even though he had a premonition that these would be harder to crack than the Old Persian.

10

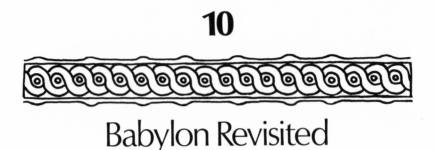

Babylon Revisited

The recovery of the Assyro-Babylonian languages was facilitated by the discovery of extensive "libraries" of cuneiform tablets in Meopotamia's forgotten cities of Babylon, Nineveh, Nimrud and others.

We have already noted that some sixteenth- and seventeenth-century travelers such as Pietro della Valle and Abbé Beauchamps had brought home a few strange, baked clay tablets covered with wedge-shaped imprints. At first, these tablets were merely regarded as curious souvenirs. No one dreamed that in the region between the Tigris and Euphrates rivers there were dusty mounds covering silent libraries crammed with stirring epics, catalogues of great laws, histories, even dictionaries and grammars. The names of the mounds had been kept alive in the Old Testament and, of course, by Herodotus, but no one bothered to look for the legendary places until the early nineteenth century. The man who initiated the search was Claudius James Rich, one of those

scholar-adventurers the British seemed to produce by the bushel.

Rich was born in Dijon, France, in 1787, of English parents. He received his early schooling in Bristol, and like so many personalities of that period who became associated with the Near East, he was a youthful prodigy. When he was nine years old he began studying Arabic, and at fourteen he took up Chinese. At sixteen he became a cadet in the service of the East Indian Company and was dispatched to India.

His journey to the East turned into a perilous saga. His first ship made calls at Mediterranean ports and was wrecked at Malta. The next boat carried him to Constantinople. Because it was dangerous for a young Briton to travel alone in that part of the world, he made good use of his accentless Arabic and his knowledge of Near Eastern customs. He disguised himself as a Mameluke, traveling on foot and by camel across Syria and Palestine to Egypt. While in Syria he even visited the great mosque at Damascus without being detected. Finally he reached Bombay where he served as a company administrator before being sent to Bagdad as a consular representative.

His duties in Bagdad were not oppressive. He had time for an occasional visit home, time to marry an English girl, time to explore much of the region between the Tigris and Euphrates. The area fascinated him because of its connection with Biblical stories, and he decided to look for ancient Babylon. The legendary city was not really lost, it was merely unrecognizable. About twenty-five miles south of Bagdad stood a large mound which was still called *Babil*.

In 1811, Rich and his young wife made their first trip to this site. The area had been plundered and razed and was so covered with the debris of ages that Rich found only scattered signs of the once mighty city. There was no tower of Babel, no vast

Detail of Babylonian cuneiform script carved in stone.
PHOTO: NORMAN, COURTESY, LOUVRE MUSEUM

palace where King Belshazzar had once made a great feast for a thousand of his lords, and where a moving finger wrote the cryptic message—*mene mene tekel upharsin*—on a wall. Nothing remained of this palace where Daniel of the Bible decoded the Aramaic words which meant, "numbered, numbered, weighed, divided," and which prophecied the destruction of Belshazzar's kingdom. Nevertheless, Rich and his wife made the most of this visit as well as later ones. They made accurate measurements, took notes, sketched and rescued some cuneiform tablets.

Although Rich died of cholera, in Shiraz, when he was only thirty-three, his two-volume book, *A Narrative of a Journey to the Site of Babylon*, aroused much interest in Europe. It is ironic, however, that this man who first focused Europe's attention on Babylon, and who write a description of it for the sixth *Encyclopedia Britannica*, is not included in many modern encyclopedias. But he was remembered, at least, by the English poet and traveler, Lord Byron, in his famous *Don Juan*: "Though Claudius Rich, Esquire, some bricks has got,/And written lately two memoirs upon't."

Rich's book excited members of the Société Asiatique in Paris. They got the French government to finance a search for cuneiform "manuscripts" and antiquities in the upper Mesopotamia region around Mosul. The man chosen for this task, and appointed French consul at Mosul, was an energetic Italian named Paul Emile Botta. He was a physician, had also served various nations as a diplomat, spoke Turkish and Arabic and was a skillful handler of men.

Although Botta feuded continually with the Turkish Pasha at Mosul (who was in charge of issuing permits allowing foreigners to travel or dig in the area) and was frequently threatened by Berber tribesmen, the Italian's skill at diplomacy and at handling men paid off. Soon he was on horseback, exploring, questioning the desert tribesmen and excavating in the numerous mounds lying in the wasteland east of Mosul and across the Tigris.

About fourteen miles from Mosul, near the village of Korsabad he located the remains of an extensive palace. In it he found valuable deposits of statuary and cuneiform tablets. He believed he had discovered Nineveh. In a message sent to the Asiatic Society in Paris, he wrote: "I believe myself to be the first who has discovered sculptures which with some reason can be referred to the period when Nineveh was flourishing."

French newspapers and magazines headlined the news. Orientalists were asked to write feature articles. Biblical students combed through the old testament for references to the storied city. Actually, Botta had not found Nineveh. He had located a kind of summer palace on the outskirts of Nineveh which had been built in 709 B.C., for the Assyrian king Sargon II.

Botta's three years of digging (1843–1846) filled the Louvre Museum in Paris with a priceless collection of carvings, statuary and, above all, numerous cuneiform tablets. In our present-day era of scientific archaeology the careless digging methods of Botta and other antiquarians of his period seem horrifying. It was like large-scale grave robbing to fill the museums of Europe. No one thought of recording the stratas, or levels, in which the treasures were located. Often there was a great deal of breakage of important artifacts just to dig out a nice museum piece. Nevertheless, despite the carelessness, men like Botta contributed to our knowledge of the lost civilizations. Botta himself produced a five-volume book excellently illustrated by the artist Flandin. It has not only become a classic but its rich collection of inscriptions helped Rawlinson and others decode the Babylonian script.

If Botta's efforts filled the Louvre, then his work was capped by a young explorer-excavator who found the real Nineveh and literally carried it to England.

In Austen Henry Layard we find, again, one of those unusual English gentlemen who never seemed to stay at home. Layard's travels began at birth. He was born in Paris in 1817 while his parents were visiting there. He received a good classical education at schools in England, France, Switzerland and Italy. As a young boy his romantic sense of adventure was whetted when he used to hide beneath a great Florentine table in his father's house and pore through stories of the *Arabian Nights.* Like Rawlinson, he had no intention of becoming a scholar or archaeologist. The East called him, but his ambition was to become a tea planter in Ceylon.

In 1839 Layard left London for the East. He first went to Constantinople, stopping there for a while to polish his Arabic and Turkish, and to visit with friends of his father. Then he followed what seemed to have become a well-beaten tourist track; he wandered from the Bosphorus to Aleppo, down to Lebanon, to Damascus, to Bagdad and, finally, to Mosul where he met Emile Botta. Like Botta, he was stirred by the mysterious mounds in the region, and he took up the work of investigating them where the Italian had left off.

Layard's diggings in Mesopotamia spanned more than a decade. In the beginning he lacked the kind of financing the Italian had received, and during a brief period he was operating on a small sixty-five-pound grant given by the British ambassador in Constantinople. He was also harried by the local Turkish Pasha, and saw his operations stopped by the petty revolutions that swept the region. Nevertheless he persisted and succeeded. During November 1845, this twenty-eight-year-old excavator made a spectacular discovery while clearing away rubble from the walls of two Assyrian palaces: he came upon a vast store of ancient art—statuary, inscriptions and some colossal winged-lions and bulls. These figures which had rested undisturbed for twenty-eight centuries were painstakingly removed from the earth, transported by rollers to the Tigris, then transported six hundred miles down river to the Persian Gulf. Reloaded on larger vessels, the huge figures were shipped twelve thousand miles to England. Today they are part of the impressive Assyrian exhibit in the British Museum.

The incredible booty that he sent home, plus the exciting book about his adventures—*Nineveh and Its Remains*, again changed Layard's career. From prospective tea planter, he shifted to archaeology, then to politics; he became, successively, the British undersecretary of foreign affairs, minister of public works and ambassador to Spain.

Layard's greatest Mesopotamian discovery, the one most important in the story of cuneiform decipherments, was made in the fall of 1849 while investigating the mound called Kayunjik, near Mosul. There he uncovered one of the great palaces of Nineveh, the Palace of Sennacherib, the bloody Assyrian king who ruled from 704 to 681 B.C. In addition to the massive sculptures, friezes and splendid mosaics, he found a "library" housing thousands of cuneiform tablets.

The library had been collected by King Assurbanipal, the son of one of Sennacherib's favorite wives. Between 688 and 662 B.C., Assurbanipal tried to round up every shred of knowledge that existed in the ancient world. He set agents out to scour his kingdom for cuneiform tablets, and he gathered together an army of scholars and "writers" who assembled a library of thirty thousand clay tablets. These "baked books" of cuneiform writing contained treatises on magic and rituals, medical works, historical accounts, philosophic and literary works. Among the tablets Layard sent home, scholars eventually found that more than one hundred of them were instruction manuals and dictionaries for Assyrian students studying cuneiform writing.*

While Botta and Layard were recovering more examples of Assyro-Babylonian texts than anyone imagined existed, Rawlinson in Bagdad, and other scholars in Europe, had finally begun to decipher the Akkadian script. Although Rawlinson had already matched the proper names in the Old Persian and the Babylonian texts copied from the Behistun Rock, he and his colleagues in Europe still encountered great difficulties.

There were more than three hundred signs in the Assyro-Babylonian cuneiforms, some with phonetic values, others that were ideograms, still others that served as determinative signs which were never pronounced. Furthermore there were many polyphonous signs, that is, a single sign that could be pronounced in several different ways, depending on the context of the sentence. (An English example: I can *read*. I have *read*.) There were also homophonous signs, that is, different signs with the same pronunciation. (English example: He went to the *polls*. He cut down telephone *poles*.) Certain combinations of vowels and consonants permitted the same word to be spelled differently, just as in English we might write *theater* and *theatre*, or *endeavor* and *endeavour*. A further complication, discovered by Botta, was that the same word might be written ideographically or syllabically; the word for "king" could be represented by a single

* During the past half-century scholars at the University of Chicago's Oriental Institute have been preparing a monumental twenty-one-volume Assyrian dictionary. The first ten volumes have just been published. This is a most remarkable project because the language has not been spoken for twenty-five hundred years and was lost for more than one thousand years.

king ideogram, or it could be spelled out with the three signs representing the sounds *sha-ar-ru*.

Henry Creswicke Rawlinson and the noted Franco-German scholar, Jules Oppert, are credited with the decipherment of the Assyro-Babylonian cuneiforms, but several other men also made important contributions to the solution. In Sweden the Semitic scholar, Isidor Löwenstern, demonstrated the Semitic character of Akkadian, revealing its relationship to Hebrew and Arabic. Thus by comparing certain words of Akkadian to these languages, their meaning or sounds could be found. Rev. Edward Hincks, an Irish clergyman in the Anglican Church, and William Henry Fox Talbot, a mathematician and inventor of Talbotype photography, also made useful discoveries.

By 1850, Rawlinson, after almost abandoning his work on the Babylonian script, finally succeeded in deciphering and translating a fairly long historical passage in Akkadian. He shared his finds with Oppert, Hincks and Talbot. Soon all three men were making incredible strides in reading the cuneiforms and discovering, to their amazement, how rich the Assyro-Babylonian literature was.

As in the case of Champollion's successful decipherment of Egyptian, the Babylonian decipherers also met with much opposition. Intelligent scholars, accustomed to reading ancient texts in languages having simple alphabets such as Greek or Latin, simply refused to believe that anyone could read something as complicated as the Akkadian cuneiforms. To prove that the wedge script from Mesopotamia was being read, William Fox Talbot proposed an unorthodox test. He suggested that Edwin Norris, secretary of the Asiatic Society in London, set up a kind of translating competition.

Norris arranged the test in 1857 when, by chance Rawlinson,

Hincks, Oppert and Fox Talbot—the four leading Assyriologists —were in London. At this same time the British Museum had just received three clay cylinders containing an edict of Assyrian King Tiglath-pileser I (1113–1074 B.C.). None of the experts had seen the cylinders. Norris had lithograph copies of the cuneiform text made. He sent them to the four scholars who, except for Fox Talbot, were not aware that others had received the same sealed envelopes. Each man worked alone, and when their translations were unsealed and examined by a committee of the Asiatic Society, it was found that all four decipherments were quite in agreement. Although some scholars (but none of the four) resented this kind of experiment, a point had been made. Men could really read Babylonian cuneiforms.

11

A Lost Civilization
and a Forgotten Flood

Men had learned to read ancient Egyptian, Old Persian and the Assyrian-Babylonian records, but the wonders were not over. They were on the verge of reading the language and literature of a civilization far older than these.

In 1850, while translating some of the countless cuneiform texts pouring into Europe from Mesopotamia, the clergyman-decipherer Edward Hincks was disturbed by certain oddities: on some of the tablets from Nineveh he found words that did not seem to belong to the Semitic language of the Assyrians. He was also disturbed by the complexity of the language; the span of Babylonian and Assyrian history was too short for such a language and script to have developed. He wondered if the script might not have been developed for another language. He passed this idea on to Jules Oppert who had already thought of the same thing.

By this time, Oppert, though he was still in his late twenties, had become one of the outstanding figures in Assyrian studies. Oppert was the son of a well-to-do Jewish family in Hamburg, Germany, and his career was similar to that of so many leading Orientalists of the period. He had set out to become a mathematician, then abandoned this calling in order to study law at Heidelberg. After receiving his doctoral degree, he studied Oriental languages at Bonn. Like Champollion, he quickly mastered Arabic, Sanskrit, Hebrew, Coptic, Old Persian, as well as a half-dozen Near Eastern dialects.

His treatise on the phonetic system of Old Persian, published in 1847, not only verified Rawlinson's findings and supported some of Hincks' discoveries, but it brought these men together in a lifelong friendship. They could often be seen together in Paris or London. When they were involved in learned discussions, the contrast between them was memorable: Hincks argued with Irish passion; Rawlinson, now a trustee of the British Museum, was taciturn; young Oppert, eyes flashing in his handsome face, argued with wit and brilliance.

Hincks had advanced the idea that the Babylonian script had been invented for another language. Oppert went further suggesting the other language might have been an Indo-European tongue rather than Semitic. But, whose language? Had an earlier culture existed in the Tigris-Euphrates valley long before the Babylonians? Drawing upon his vast knowledge of Eastern languages and comparative philology, Oppert was able to show how the cuneiform script had been adapted to the Akkadian language.

In the manner of modern astronomers who are able to predict the eventual discovery of a planet which no telescope has yet located, simply on the basis of irregularities in the orbit of known planets, Jules Oppert predicted that a lost civilization would be found. He gave these forgotten people a name—Sumerian. He chose the name from a text on a cuneiform tablet Layard had found at Nineveh; it had mentioned the title used by the earliest known ruler of southern Mesopotamia, a man who had called himself "King of Sumer and Akkad."

Although Oppert was supported by Hincks and Rawlinson, many scholars refused to accept the daring hypothesis. There was no physical proof, no revealing excavations. Even classical historians such as Herodotus, who had traveled in Mesopotamia and had described Babylon so vividly, mentioned no such older civiliiazton. And the Bible, which recorded struggles between the Jews and the Assyrian-Babylonian peoples, told of no older culture, unless it might have been a passing mention of "the land of Shinar" where descendants of Noah had built a city. But the scientific minds of the nineteenth century no longer regarded the Old Testament as sound history. Proof was needed—tangible proof of ruins or temples. The doubters, of course, ignored some evidence that lay right under their noses. In the great store of cuneiform "books" which had been brought from Nineveh, scholars had found bilingual vocabularies, bilingual grammatical exercises and bilingual translations. On these tablets one of the columns of cuneiform was Akkadian-Semitic, the parallel column was in the language Oppert had named "Sumerian." During this lively controversy (whether there was a Sumerian language or not), one of Europe's leading scholars, Joseph Halévy, bitterly opposed Oppert. He argued that there was no such language, that it was merely an esoteric script used by Babylonian priests and magicians to hide their secrets from prying eyes.

Jules Oppert held his ground. He said that the desert regions of southern Mesopotamia had hardly been explored, that it was virgin ground awaiting the spade and brush of curious archaeologists. His beliefs began to be confirmed when explorers uncovered mounds at Warka and Tell el-Muquayyar in the 1850s. Reading a cylinder inscription from the Nineveh "library," Rawlinson identified Tell el-Muquayyar as the ancient Sumerian city of Ur, and archaeologists found there pottery, statuary and other relics which Oppert quickly noted as being quite different in style than anything found in the Assyrian and Babylonian digs.

Between 1877 and 1900 the French archaeologist Ernest de Sarzac added to the evidence. He located the Sumerian city of Lagash and recovered splendid archaic statues and a quantity of Sumerian cuneiform tablets. Then the greatest store of Sumerian inscriptions was recovered by archaeologists from the University of Pennsylvania while excavating at Nippur. They found a "library" of thirty thousand cuneiform tablets, two thousand of which were Sumerian literary texts, including an amazing Sumerian account of the Deluge.

A brief account of the discovery of the Gilgamesh Epic and the Babylonian-Sumerian story of the Flood should be given here because it was an important episode in the decipherment of the cuneiform scripts.

When Layard abandoned archaeology for a political career, the British Museum asked Hormuzd Rassam, his assistant, to continue with the excavations at Nineveh. Rassam, an Oxford-educated, Chaldean Christian who had been born at Mosul, and who had already had an exciting career as a British interpreter and diplomatic messenger in the Near East, immediately uncovered another "library" room at Nineveh. He shipped the clay tablets to England. Naturally, he did not know that among them there was a large fragment which would soon shake the entire Christian world.

The man who discovered the importance of this find was

George Smith, a self-educated Assyriologist who did most of his digging in the British Museum basement. Smith had been born in London, March 16, 1840, to a family that could not afford to send him to higher schools. Since he showed a knack for drawing he was apprenticed to a Bouverie Street engraver. He became so skilled at this he was promoted to the exacting job of engraving bank notes.

Making money that did not belong to him was somewhat boring so he began spending his lunch hours at the Museum. The engravedlike cuneiform wedges interested him. Soon he was spending both lunch hour and evenings reading everything available about Mesopotamia and studying cuneiform scripts. When he was twenty-one, he was noticed by Samuel Birch, the Keeper of the Museum, who hired him as an assistant restorer. He was assigned to the Assyrian section, where soon he not only was expertly fitting broken cuneiform tablets together, but was also reading the difficult script as well as most highly trained professionals. Rawlinson was so impressed by Smith's grasp of the Akkadian language that he invited the young man to use his personal workshop in the museum and to assist in cataloging the Nineveh tablets. Smith quickly proved his worth by recovering from a tablet the date of the eclipse of the sun over Nineveh in 763 B.C. A short while later, he fixed the date of the Elamite invasion of Babylonia at 2280 B.C.

One day, while reading the clay tablets Hormuzd Rassam had sent from Nineveh, he noticed that one of the texts was an exceptionally long literary one. It appeared to be an epic poem and was called *sa nagba imuru*, meaning "He who saw everything."

It recounted the adventures of a part divine, part human, ancient hero named Gilgamesh. After a variety of encounters with gods, enemies and mythical beasts, Gilgamesh tries to find the secret of eternal life, and he calls upon the spirit of his ancestor, Ut-Napish-tim for advice. Ut-Napishtim philosophizes about the uncertainties of life and tells him about a great flood which only he survived.

As George Smith read the lines they seemed to echo familiarly in his head:

> *. . . Son of Ubar-tutu,*
> *Tear down thy house, build an ark!*
> *Give up possessions, seek thou life.*
> *Despise property and keep thy soul alive!*
> *Aboard the ship take thou the seed of all living*
> *things.**

Smith slowly translated the text, reading how the ship was built and caulked with pitch, then how a great deluge engulfed the earth. The sluices of the sky opened and everything human was transformed into mud. Ut-Napishtim's ark drifted for six days and seven nights, then the flood subsided, and,

> *On Mount Nisir the ark came to a halt.*
> *Mount Nisir held the ship fast,*
> *Allowing no motion . . .*

Then Ut-Napishtim tells Gilgamesh:

> *When the seventh day arrived,*
> *I sent forth and set free a dove.*

George Smith was stunned. Was this, on Assyrian tablets, the same story of the Flood that was told in the Bible? For a moment he wondered if he had translated this or had dreamed it. He sent a messenger for Rawlinson.

---

* The translation of *The Epic of Gilgamesh* appearing in this chapter is by E. A. Speiser, included in *Ancient Near Eastern Texts* (Princeton, N.J.: Princeton University Press, 1950).

When Rawlinson carefully read Smith's translation, comparing it with the cuneiform he confirmed the younger man's work. He, likewise, was tremendously excited. Then he noticed something that Smith had also noted; the Deluge story broke off before its end. A part of the tale was missing. The two men reviewed the text on the ten other tablets making up the Gilgamesh Epic. No, they had not read the "clay books" in the wrong order. The Flood account appeared on the eleventh tablet. Was there a twelfth tablet, or a fragment of one, with the missing conclusion? Although all the Nineveh tablets had been carefully catalogued, the storerooms of the museum were again searched without success.

"If it exists, it must still be at Nineveh," Smith said.

On the evening of December 3, 1872, Smith read a full report of his discovery to the London Society of Biblical Archaeology. The auditorium was jammed because rumors had circulated about the sensational nature of the revelation. Important dignitaries and scholars including Rawlinson and Prime Minister Gladstone were on the platform. After describing his discovery, George Smith found that he had become famous overnight. His treatise rocked Victorian England and, in a short time, the rest of the world.

Rationalists in Europe and America used it as an argument to support their contention that the Old Testament was not divinely inspired scripture. It proved that the Hebrew story about Noah and the Flood was borrowed from an earlier literature. And as far as the Deluge was concened, it probably was not an historical fact; it was merely an ancient myth. Other people, however, were more interested in the Gilgamesh Epic itself. Could the missing portion of the Deluge story be found?

At the Biblical Society meeting, Smith had mentioned that the missing fragment might be found in Mesopotamia. He estimated there were about fifteen lines missing. This unusual surmise so tickled the owner of the *London Daily Telegraph* that the newspaper offered a prize of £1,000 to the person who found the missing tablet.

The British Museum's directors thought they might send a man on this rare quest. First they thought an archaeologist should go, but, on further reflection, they realized that if anyone were to find the missing lines, the man must be able to read Babylonian cuneiforms, and he must be so familiar with the text that he would recognize it on sight. The natural choice was George Smith.

Although he had hardly traveled beyond London, he set out immediately on the long voyage the length of the Mediterranean, across Turkey to Aleppo, then down the rivers of Mesopotamia to Mosul. His book, *Assyrian Discoveries*, is filled with keen descriptions of the land, unique impressions of its people, and tales of fascinating narrow escapes from danger. The following short passage suggests its flavor: "At Djezireh, I saw a madman wandering about the streets perfectly naked, and we were annoyed here by some dancing boys, a race of professionals peculiar to Turkey. In the night, some Turkish soldiers turned our horses out of the stalls, and carried off some of the horse gear."

Arriving at Mosul, he ran into the same problems which had so plagued Botta and Layard. The Turkish Pasha refused him permission to even look at the ruins of Nineveh. It was not until mid-May, three months after he had left England, that he was finally granted the *firmin* ("permit") to work there.

On May 13, while inspecting a large pit where workmen were quarrying stone for the Mosul bridge construction, he uncovered some cuneiform tablets in a pile of rubbish. He took them back to the hut he used as his headquarters. The following day, as soon as it was light, be began dusting the fragments. The improbable occurred! "On cleaning one of them," he wrote home that evening, "I found to my surprise and gratification the greater portion of the lines belonging to the Chaldean account of the

Deluge." As he held the fragile tablet and read it in the morning light his fingers trembled. He could almost hear Ut-Napishtim telling Gilgamesh:

The dove came forth, but came back;
There was no resting place for her and she returned.
Then I sent forth and set free a swallow.
The swallow went forth and came back . . .

And the poem continues on until finally:

A raven went forth and, seeing the waters diminished,
He eats, circles, caws and turns not around.

This was an amazing feat that may never be repeated in the history of literary archaeology. What incredible confidence! George Smith had predicted he would find a fifteen-line portion of a text that had been lost for thousands of years. He had journeyed countless leagues over forbidding country to search for a small baked brick, never knowing whether it had been destroyed by the elements, by marauders or early grave robbers. He had to search for it in the sand-covered rubble of a ruined city which covered eight miles in circuit. It was like searching for a needle in a haystack that measured miles across and extended back centuries in time.

Smith collected more cuneiform tablets, then started out for England with his treasure. At Aleppo the boxes of carefully packed tablets were presented at the Turkish Custom Office for clearance. Smith had with him an official letter from the Pasha at Mosul, which he believed was an authorization to take the material out of the country. He found, instead, that he had been tricked by the annoying Pasha. The letter contained orders to stop the shipment. "They made me the bearer of a letter directed against myself," he observed with irony.

After much negotiating the rare collection was finally sent to the British Museum. Meanwhile, the spell of the desert country and the excitement of exploration fell upon George Smith. London appeared pale and dull, so he returned to the Near East to hunt for more cuneiform records. In 1876, while journeying across the arid region between Mesopotamia and Aleppo, he was struck down by cholera. The last entry in his diary, written in a weak scrawl, was dated August 12. "I am not well. If we had a doctor here, I'm sure I should be all right. But he hasn't come. If I die, farewell . . ." Six days later he died in Aleppo.

During his short lifetime Smith not only found and translated one of mankind's great ancient epics from clay tablets which had been inscribed during the eighth century B.C., but he had established brilliantly the relationship between the Old Testament and the Gilgamesh story. Ut-Napishtim was none other than the Biblical Noah. Although he knew that his discovery had shaken Victorian England, the chain reaction initiated by it might have surprised him.

After Smith's death, University of Pennsylvania scholars working at Nippur, the religious center of the Sumerians, found much older copies of the same epic. These date back to about 1500 B.C. And authorities now believe the poem itself is much older, existing as a spoken epic before 3000 B.C. An even more startling link in the chain was discovered by the noted English archaeologist, Sir Leonard Woolley.

During the 1920s Woolley began excavating at Tell el-Muquayyar, uncovering the ancient Sumerian city of Ur. Some five thousand years ago it had been a flourishing port at the head of the Persian Gulf. Now, because the shoreline of the gulf has receded over the centuries, it stands 100 miles inland. During its long existence it was built and rebuilt, occupied by Sumerians, by Assyrio-Babylonians and by the Biblical Chaldeans. It was the birthplace of Abraham. As Woolley and his men uncovered the numerous layers and kept digging deeper and systematically into the Sumerian past, they came upon a startling stratum of clay. It was about forty feet down and was almost eight and a half feet thick. It separated an older city from later constructions. What was remarkable about this thick clay deposit is that it was pure clay, completely free of man-made rubbish and pottery shards. Geologists who have studied it are of the opinion that it could only have been laid down by an enormous inundation of the land of Sumer, a tremendous deluge caused by unusual rains, making the Tigris and Euphrates overflow their banks, raising huge tides that swept in from the gulf across the Tigris estuary.

Thus it appears that the story of a great Deluge, told in the ancient Gilgamesh epic and retold in the Old Testament, was not myth but an historical fact.

Just as the decipherment of Egyptian hieroglyphics pushed back man's history helping us understand the origins of many of our beliefs and customs, so too the decipherment of the wedge-shaped cuneiforms has let us look even farther back.

Although Mesopotamia may seem distant from the United States or Europe, we are still linked by the thin thread of history to people who lived ages ago in distant Ur and Babylon. The Sumerians were the first to devise the day we still observe as the Sabbath, Sunday or the seventh day of rest. They invented a calendar of four-week "months" of twenty-eight days, with each seventh day reserved for rest.

About 2100 B.C., the Sumerians decided it would be useful to organize the laws governing populations into a system so that they could be applied fairly and uniformly. Around 1800 B.C., the Babylonian ruler, Hammurabi, systemized the laws into a memorable, written code of nearly three hundred paragraphs. Although justice was harsh, this code was quite modern because it insisted that the state should be the dispenser of justice, rather than letting individuals avenge wrongdoings.

Modern-day stockbrokers and bankers may believe that our ideas about capital, interest and investments are fairly new, but they really date back to Babylonia. Law No. 102 in the Hammurabi Code says: "If a merchant lends money to a trader without interest, and the trader's enterprise fails, the trader need only return the principal since there is no profit to share."

Even some of the high-finance terms we use had their origins in the Near East. For example, the following cuneiform glyphs, pronounced *qá-qá-ad* in Akkadian, actually meant "head." But in the

Assyrian signs, about 700 B.C., meaning "principal" or "capital."

commercial world of Babylonia and Assyria it also signified something invested, some principal or capital, lent to someone in order to make a profit. In other Near Eastern languages as well as Greek the term for "capital" is related to "head." We can also trace our Western usage of the term from the Latin word *caput*, meaning "head" or "the capital of a column."

The science of astronomy and mathematics, begun by the Sumerians, reached a high level of development in the Assyrian-Babylonian kingdoms. Priest-astronomers predicted eclipses of the sun and moon and mapped the movements of the planets. They invented a kind of antique slide rule or reckoning table to do involved calculations. In architecture they developed the principle of the arch. And in the area of religion, many of our traditional beliefs, long thought to date back to Hebraic scriptures, are now known to have originated in the early civilizations of the Tigris-Euphrates valley.

12

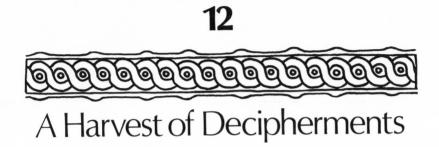

A Harvest of Decipherments

The great classical decipherments of the first half of the nineteenth century made people in the United States and Europe well aware of the ancient history of the Near East, but for many years they believed there had been only two important civilizations in that region—the Egyptian and the many-layered cultures in Mesopotamia. Then, between the 1870s and the early years of the twentieth century, a growing army of explorers, linguists and decipherers uncovered a new crop of forgotten civilizations and languages. It was as if someone had knifed through an onion, revealing layer after layer of cultures and tongues that had been lost to human memory.

They soon began to realize how complex the civilizations of the Near East had been. There were dozens of languages spoken: Hittite, Hattic, Luwian, Palaian, Hurrian, Urartaean, Elamite, Ugaritic, Lycian-Lydian, Carian, Numidian, Meroitic, and more. Some of these represented important civilizations while others served as the distinctive languages and writing systems of less influential cultures. For their writing they used variations of the cuneiform script and Egyptianlike hieroglyphics. In origin many of the languages were Semitic, some were Indo-European (a family of languages including most European, Slavic and Indo-Iranian tongues), while the origins of a few are still unrecognized.

Since the list is long, we shall limit this chapter to telling how two major ancient languages and their civilizations were discovered and deciphered. At chapter's end we'll include a short description of the other scripts and how far their writing has been decoded.

The most impressive Near Eastern culture, paralleling the Egyptian and the Assyro-Babylonian was that of the Hittite people who dominated a region extending from central Turkey to Palestine. During the fourteenth and fifteenth centuries B.C. the Hittite empire rivaled those of Egypt and Mesopotamia. The Hittite capital, Hattusas, in central Turkey (near present-day Boghazköy, ninety-five miles east of Ankara), was noted for its culture and lively commerce. It was destroyed by invaders in the early twelfth century B.C. The language of these people is the oldest recorded Indo-European tongue and is related to Sanskrit, Greek, Latin and most well-known European languages.

It is ironic that the Hittites, though they ruled over a great empire and produced a rich literature, were almost as completely forgotten as the Sumerians. They were, of course, mentioned a half-dozen times in the Bible. Solomon, for example, took Hittite wives and "bought horses from Egypt for all the kings of the Hittites, and for the kings of Syria . . ." But during the nineteenth century the Old Testament was considered an unreliable history until the decipherments of Champollion and Rawlinson helped us see deeper into the past.

The man who first noticed that there might be a Hittite language was a scholar-adventurer known as Sheikh Ibrahim. He was usually addressed as "Hadji," a title reserved for men who had made the pilgrimage to Mecca. When he died in 1817, he was buried in the Moslem cemetery at Cairo with all the honors due to a high-ranking Mohammedan. Actually, Sheikh Hadji Ibrahim was a Swiss-born scholar, Johann Ludwig Burckhardt, who had studied Arabic in Germany and England, who had become a British citizen and who was a representative of the British African Society in the Near East.

Burckhardt was so at home in Arabic that, after having been examined by Mohammedan scholars, he was permitted to visit the forbidden shrines at Mecca and Medina. Between 1809 and 1817 he traveled widely through Syria, Lebanon, Jordan and Egypt, usually going disguised as an Arab merchant. In the course of his wanderings he visited the Syrian town of Hama (the Hamath of the Old Testament) where he noticed a stone covered with pictographs and hieroglyphs which appeared unlike the Egyptian signs. He gave a brief description of the strange glyphs in his *Travels in Syria and the Holy Land*, published by the London Royal Geographical Society five years after his death.

No one paid any attention to his commentary until the Hamath Stone and four similar ones were rediscovered sixty years later, and copies were sent to the British Museum. Soon more examples of the same hieroglyphic script were found in central Turkey and in Egypt. The decipherment of Egyptian made scholars even more aware of the Hittites. In a temple at Karnak the text of a treaty between the Egyptian Pharaoh Ramses II and the Hittite King Hattusilis III was found. Then, in 1887, at Tell el-Amarna in Egypt a number of tablets were discovered. These were letters that had been enchanged between Hittite and Egyptian kings; among

Section of carved Hittite hieroglyphics found at Hama in Syria by
Ludwig Burckhardt. PHOTO: NORMAN

them were two letters in a curious cuneiform script which was given the name "Arzawa."

As more scholars became involved in Hittite studies, they realized that these people had two systems of writing: the Hittites had adapted the Assyro-Babylonian cuneiforms to their tongue (the "Arzawa" script), but they also wrote an odd form of hieroglyphics. The cuneiform type of writing went out of vogue after the collapse of the empire in the early twelfth century B.C., but the hieroglyphic script was still used by the city-states on the fringe of the empire until the end of the eighth century when Assyrians began to dominate their region.

Although Hadji Burckhardt had discovered one of the Hittite scripts, the man who was most responsible for "rehabilitating" the Hittite civilization and preparing the way for others to decipher the two scripts was a Welch clergyman-explorer, Archibald Henry Sayce.

Sayce was a natural linguist. At age ten, he was reading Homer and Virgil in Greek and Latin. Eight years later he had mastered Hebrew, Egyptian, Persian and Sanskrit. Receiving a scholarship at Oxford, he specialized in philology and Babylonian cuneiforms. Though he remained at Oxford for sixty-three years, heading the studies in comparative philology and Assyriology, he was no armchair scholar. He traveled widely and frequently. He was perfectly at home in the deserts of the Near East and, later, in Borneo and among the islands of the Pacific. The natives of Arabia admired him and were amused because no matter where he went, or how hot it was, he always wore his clerical costume. They called him the "crazy priest," or "the father with the flat turban."

After painstakingly pooling all the information that had trickled in from the Near East, Sayce had a flash of intuition which identified the extent and importance of the Hittite empire. In his *Reminiscences* he describes this brilliant moment which occurred while visiting a friend, Isaac Taylor.

> One morning I was with him in his library when the question of the so-called Hamathite inscriptions turned up. These were inscriptions in a new form of hieroglyphic script which had first been detected on certain stones at Hamath. . . . While I was talking to Taylor a sudden inspiration came to me. I asked him for a copy of Rawlinson's Herodotus, and then pointed out to him that a picture in it of a monument in the pass of Karabel near Smyrna . . .

The two men studied the photograph, comparing it to other photographs and Hittite-like hieroglyphics found at Ivriz and at Carchemish. Sayce continues:

> they belonged to the same school of art as certain figures cut on the rocks of an ancient sanctuary near Boghaz Keui [Boghazköy] in Cappadocia. . . . we saw that not only was the art the same at Boghaz Keui, at Karabel, at Ivriz and at Carchemish, but that the figures of Boghaz Keui were accompanied by hieroglyphs similar to those at Ivriz. It was clear that in pre-hellenic days a powerful empire must have existed in Asia Minor which extended from the Aegean to the Halys and southward into Syria, to Carchemish and Hamath, and possessed its own special artistic culture and its own special script. And so the story of the Hittite empire was introduced to the world.

Sayce's theory was not accepted immediately, but he stubbornly defended his ideas. He was sure that Boghaz Keui might be the site of the ancient Hittite capital. He was anxious for the British to excavate there. To his disappointment, German Assyriologists had more influence with the Turkish government, and they were given permission to work in the area.

The discoveries made by the 1906–1908 expedition of Berlin's Dr. Hugo Winkler dramatically proved the correctness of Sayce's ideas. Boghazköy was, indeed, the site of ancient Hattusas. In its ruins Winckler found the royal archives of the Hittites, bringing to light ten thousand cuneiform tablets, most of them written in "Arzawa," which was nothing more than Hittite. The archives also included clay tablets written in other languages—Akkadian, Sumerian, Hurrian and several unknown scripts. These reflected the multinational character of the Hittite capital and its empire.

With such an enormous supply of tablets available, decipherers could now try to crack the Hittite scripts. Since the cuneiform examples were more plentiful, the first successful attack began with them. Decipherers were working with a known script and an unknown language.

At first there were delays because most scholars believed the language was related in some way to the Semitic tongue of the Assyrians and Babylonians. In 1902 a Norwegian Assyriologist, J. A. Knudtzon, suggested that the language might be Indo-European in origin rather than Semitic. So many specialists attacked this idea that Knudtzon finally backed down. Nevertheless, after Winkler's discovery of the Hittite archives, a young Bohemian linguist, Bedřich Hrozný, revived Knudtzon's concept and succeeded in deciphering the cuneiform script.

Hrozný, born in 1897, developed an interest in Near Eastern languages and history while studying theology. He had learned Arabic, Hebrew and Akkadian, languages which won him not only a post as librarian at the University of Vienna but also a commission to go to Constantinople in order to prepare copies of the Boghazköy tablets for publication. On returning to Vienna, he began puzzling over the Hittite scripts.

One day, while letting his imagination and his keen sense of word combinations play freely over a long text, he came upon a passage consisting of two parallel halves which balanced each other, the endings of each half rhyming. This, he knew, was one of the characteristics of early Oriental languages. He identified the cuneiform symbols and translated their phonetic values into the Latin alphabet, producing the following lines:

nu ninda en e-iz-za-at-te-ni
wa-a-tar-ma e-ku-ut-te-ni

He recognized the Sumerian-Babylonian ideogram, *ninda*, which meant "bread." Then he experienced a flash of inspiration. It was as if the impulses in his brain were leaping about as swiftly as electrical currents through the circuits of a computer. He asked himself what verb usually goes with the word *bread*. He thought of the German word *essen*, meaning meaning "to eat." He thought of the same word in Greek, *édein*, and in Latin, *edere*. These were all Indo-European in origin. Now, glancing at the second line, the term *wa-a-tar* struck a note in his imagination. Was it related to the German *wasser*, the old Saxon *watar* and the English *water*?

Pushing this idea even further, he wondered if *e-ku-ut-te-ni* might not mean "drink." Scanning other cuneiform texts, he soon noted that the sign for *teni* appeared to be a verb ending, and that the suffix *an* seemed to indicate an accusative case (much like the Greek -*n*). He also interpreted the *nu* and the *ma* as meaning "now . . . then . . ." or "both . . . and . . ."

The solution seemed so simple it frightened him. Nevertheless, he translated the passage as: "Now you will eat bread and drink water."

This short sentence, arrived at through a flash of inspiration, became one of the decisive keys in unlocking the wealth of a forgotten language. It is very similar to the part played by the Ptolemy-Cleopatra cartouche in Champollion's decipherment of the Egyptian, or how the Darius-Xerxes sequence served as a key to the cuneiform solutions of Grotefend and Rawlinson. Once Hrozný had found his key, he was able to translate other texts. In a short while he and other scholars made such swift progress with the Hittite cuneiform script that we now have good grammars and dictionaries to assist us in mastering this first-recorded Indo-European tongue.

Hittite hieroglyphics, however, proved more difficult to decipher. When Sayce tried solving them in the early 1870s, he was confronted with the problem of an unknown language in an unknown script. Although he did establish the meanings of a handful of the ideograms and identify a few grammatical endings, he failed to realize that the language itself was Indo-European and not Semitic.

It has not been until recently, the 1930s, that a group of scholars in various countries have begun to make sense of the Hittite hieroglyphics. Their methods are too complex to describe here, but their names should be mentioned. They are: Piero Mariggi, a linguist who has worked at the University of Hamburg and at Pavia; Ignace J. Gelb, a Polish scholar connected with the Oriental Institute at the University of Chicago; the Swiss linguist, Emil Forrer; R. C. Thompson of Great Britain; and the German scholar, Helmut Theodor Bossert.

In the story of Near Eastern civilizations and the decipherment of their scripts, an unusual kind of record was set in this century when a forgotten script was discovered. The writing system and the language, Ugaritic, was first found in 1929; it was successfully deciphered in 1930.

Today we know that this language was used by the Canaanites, a Semitic people virtually identical with the Phoenicians. They dominated some four hundred miles of the Mediterranean coast from Turkey to the Negev of Palestine. The script takes its name from the city of Ugarit (a somewhat less prominent Phoenician seaport than Tyre, Sidon or Byblos). Situated at an important trading and cultural crossroad, Ugarit was a polyglot port, a Mediterranean Hong Kong of the mid-second milennium B.C. It welcomed craftsmen, traders and ambassadors from the Greek isles and mainland, Sumerians and Babylonians from Mesopotamia, Numidians and Egyptians from Africa. In its ample library, texts have been found in a dozen languages—clay tablets using wedge-shaped cuneiforms to express the native Ugaritic, Sumerian tablets for recording legal documents, Akkadian cuneiforms (for this was the international diplomatic language), Hittite cuneiforms, Egyptian hieroglyphics, and several other languages.

The history of Ugarit was long. It was occupied in the third millennium B.C. by the Canaanites. During the age of Hammurabi it was dominated by the Babylonians, but when their power diminished, the Egyptians of the Twelfth Dynasty took over. A little later the Indo-European speaking Hurrians controlled the city, but were ousted again by the Egyptians of the Eighteenth Dynasty. It is curious, however, that though so many peoples of the ancient world wanted to control Ugarit, the memory of the language and the place faded completely from human memory. Its name first came to the attention of modern readers when the so-called Arzawa cuneiform letters from Tell el-Amarna were deciphered. But no one knew where its ruins were hidden.

Ugarit was discovered by accident. In 1928 a Syrian farmer, plowing a field near Ras Shamra (Fennel Head), about ten miles north of Latakia, uncovered an ancient tomb which archaeologists at first identified as belonging to the Greek Mycenaean culture. The following year a French expedition directed by Claude Schaeffer and George Chenet began excavating the series of mounds, finding the ruins of habitations at various levels, and tombs which compared to the royal tombs in Egypt and Crete. These were described as "tombs that had contained the bodies of a princely dynasty, as yet unknown." Soon a palace was uncovered, then—a library. Professor Schaeffer described it handsomely:

> Here we have brought to light a building of large dimensions and very fine construction in freestone, with a wide entrance and an interior court, provided with wells and conduits for rain. Around this court were ranged paved chambers, with a staircase leading to an upper story. Scattered among the ruins we found quantities of large tablets covered with cuneiform texts, sometimes in three or four columns. . . . Certain fragments of a scribe's exercises showed us that we have to do here with an actual school, dependent on the adjacent temple, where young priests learned the difficult craft of the scribe and the various languages in use at Ras Shamra.

Some of the first tablets examined bore a cuneiform script somewhat like the Babylonian signs, but Schaeffer noted a distinct difference. The Ugaritic script consisted of no more than thirty characters which were simple in form. There seemed to be no determinative signs. All this suggested that the writing was not ideogrammatic or syllabic like the Akkadian system, but might be alphabetic, like the early Persian.

Charles Virolleaud of Sorbonne University and director of French Archaeological Studies in Lebanon and Syria promptly prepared and published copies of the first forty-eight tablets so that scholars everywhere might work on the newly discovered script. In an article published in the journal *Syria*, he laid the foundations for the astonishingly swift decipherment of Ugaritic. He noted the limited number of signs, that the script ran from left to right, that there were no word dividers and that there were almost no vowels.

During April 1930, copies of the text on the forty-eight tablets were delivered to Hans Bauer, son of a Grasmannsdorf innkeeper who had become Germany's leading authority on Semitic languages and history. Bauer's background was rather unusual. He had studied philosophy at the Gregorian Papal University in Rome. Then he had become an able hospital administrator. During these years he turned himself into a multilinguist; he read all the modern European languages, plus Chinese, Malayan, Korean, ancient Greek, Arabic, Old Persian, Hebrew and Assyro-Babylonian. During World War I he had served in the German army as an expert code breaker.

Bauer carefully studied the texts he had received and quickly decided that Ugaritic must be a Semitic tongue. He felt it must share certain of the structural and grammatical features found in such languages. He then applied some techniques of the cryptographer to the puzzle. Frequency counts helped him work out the sound value of many of the signs. On April 27, after a few days of intense labor, he succeeded in deciphering some of the texts. Almost on his own, without bilingual aids, he had correctly determined the value of seventeen characters.

This amazing solution was further refined by another World War I code breaker, Edouard Dhorme, who had served with the French army. Dhorme assigned phonetic values to still other letters.

Finally, on October 24, 1930, after coordinating the work of Bauer and Dhorme, Professor Virolleaud presented their solutions—a workable decipherment of one of the world's oldest alphabets—to the French Academy of Inscriptions and Belles Lettres. Since then it has been shown that this ancient alphabet evolved at about the same time, and in the same region as the "letter" alphabet which Phoenician traders spread through the Aegean and Mediterranean world. Although the forms or signs of these alphabets look quite different they are all related.

The progress that had been made in uncovering the rich art and the literature of Ugarit has proven to be one of the most important literary developments of the twentieth century. We now know that many of the Old Testament stories can be found in Canaanite texts. The Ras Shamra writings are presently helping scholars understand puzzling passages in Hebrew literature that can only be explained by knowing the Canaanite background.

The Lesser-Known Near East Languages and Scripts

ELAMITE: A cuneiform script, one of the three languages often found in the Old Persian bilinguals. The tongue of the Elamite people was not related to any well-known language, and the script's decipherment has lagged behind the successes achieved with Akkadian and Old Persian. The language is syllabic and there are no word dividers. Some fifty Elamite names have been read and the phonetic values of many of its signs are known. The most important work in deciphering it has been done by Niels Westergaard of Denmark and Edwin Norris of the Royal Asiatic Society in London.

HATTIC: The language of the pre-Hittite inhabitants of the Mediterranean coastal region. Some Hattic phrases are included in Hittite religious rituals. These and a few Hittite-Hattic bilinguals provide the only clues we have to this language.

LUWIAN and PALAIAN: Both Indo-European, both related to Hittite. So few examples of their cuneiform scripts exist that there seems to be no immediate possibility of interpreting them.

HURRIAN: An important kingdom in northwest Mesopotamia during the second millennium B.C. Linguists call the language "outlandish" and difficult to decipher because it is unrelated to Semitic, Indo-European or Sumerian. The written language is phonetic and uses Akkadian cuneiforms but very few ideographs. Numerous Hurrian texts have been found at Ugarit, Boghazköy and El Amarna. Considerable progress has been made in its decipherment.

URARTAEANS: An Armenian people who dominated the region where Turkey, Iran, Iraq and the Soviet Union meet. They are considered a younger kinfolk of the Hurrians. From the ninth to the seventh century B.C., the Urartaeans rivaled Assyrian power. They employed a late Akkadian cuneiform script.

LYCIAN and LYDIAN: Two related cultures that flourished along the southwest coast of Asia Minor about the fourth century B.C. Both used scripts that seem related to the Greek alphabet. Not enough samples of their scripts have been found to determine whether their languages were Indo-European.

CARIAN: A province between Lydia and Lycia. Although a few Greek and Carian bilinguals were found, they have not helped in cracking this still enigmatic tongue.

SIDETIC: The language of the city-kingdom of Side in Pamphylia on the southern coast of Asia Minor. Side flourished during the fifth and fourth centuries B.C. Recently discovered bilingual texts in Greek and Sidetic may help solve this script.

MERIOTIC: The script of the kingdom of Meroë, to the south of Egypt. This Ethiopian empire flourished between the first century B.C. to the fourth century A.D. In their writing the Meroës employed Egyptian hieroglyphics as well as its cursive and demotic forms. Unlike Egyptian, the language appears to have been alphabetic because only twenty-four signs were used. Twentieth-century cryptographers have begun to solve this script.

NUMIDIAN: The language of ancient Numidia (present-day Algeria and Tunisia). The Numidians were a Berber people who were originally dependent on Carthage, but during the second Punic War (218–201 B.C.) the Numidians received Roman support and built a mighty empire in North Africa. They evolved an alphabetic, consonantal script. A modification of this writing is still used by the Tuareg desert tribes.

13

New-World Writing

While the wonders of ancient Egypt were being revealed to Europe by the survivors of Napoleon's ill-fated campaign along the Nile, a German baron was busily rediscovering forgotten civilizations in the New World.

We use the word *rediscover* because shortly after the memorable voyage of Christopher Columbus, Spaniards found that the great American double continent was well-peopled and that numerous high cultures had developed. Explorers met the powerful Aztecs in central Mexico; they encountered remnants of the Maya civilization in Yucatán and Central America; they fought with the Inca in western South America. Nevertheless after less than one hundred years of contact, even intermarriage, with the conquered people the Europeans virtually forgot that such civilizations had ever existed. Ancient cities of the New World which had once housed as many as one hundred thousand souls were shrouded by the debris of time. Jaguars prowled the deserted corridors of empty palaces. And the writings of these civilizations were hidden by jungle growths or, more often than not, in the musty stacks of European libraries and monasteries.

The early discoverers of this other world must have been as awed on first seeing it as Napoleon's infantrymen were when they gazed at the silent Sphinx. The first European contact with one of the civilizations was an accidental one. In 1517 Francisco Hernández de Córdoba, commanding a slave-hunting, exploring expedition from the Spanish base at Cuba, was caught in a violent storm and blown upon an uncharted shore. It was Mexico's Peninsula of Yucatán. To the amazement of Córdoba and his men, a stone city with terraced pyramids and palace buildings seemed to rise above the flat land, some two leagues from the sea. The city was inhabited by people who wore colorful garments and decorated the walls of their temples and monuments with splendid jaguar-and-serpent bas-reliefs and strange glyphlike writing.

This voyage initiated the exploration of Mexico. A year later another search of the coastline was made by Juan de Grijalva. Finally, in 1519, Hernando Cortés launched his fabulous conquest of the Mexican heartland. When the conquistador first landed at Veracruz, he was met by ambassadors of the Aztec ruler Moctezuma, and they presented him two books written in the native picture-script (usually called a *codex* or *codice*). Cortés sent them to his sovereign, Charles I.

Learned men in the Spanish court were amused by the books; they mistook the curious signs to be designs for embroidery. One man disagreed. He was Peter Martyr (Pietro Martire Vermigli), a scholarly Florentine churchman who later became a leader in the Protestant Reformation. Martyr had traveled in Egypt and had seen hieroglyphics. He believed the Mexican codices were authentic texts in an unknown script, perhaps as impossible to read as the mysterious Egyptian writing. We don't know on what grounds he based this, but he suggested that the symbolic writing probably dealt with astronomical observations and religious ceremonies. He was quite right.

One of Cortés' companions, Bernal Díaz del Castillo, also took note of the Aztec system of writing and keeping records. In his exciting *True History of the Conquest of New Spain*, Bernal Díaz mentioned that while he was at Zempoala, a Totonac city near the coast, he saw many paper books "doubled together in folds like the cloth of Castile." Later, in the Aztec capital, Tenochtitlán (now Mexico City), he visited the archives and record offices where the Aztec revenues were "kept in books made of a paper which they called *amatl.*"

The Indian books or codices were sometimes made of deer skin, but most of them were made of long strips of parchmentlike paper that was folded like an accordian. The paper was manufactured from the inner bark of the amate tree, a native fig. The bark was soaked, beaten and pressed into long flat sheets, then the surface was sized with a coating of gum and a final coating of gesso. *Amatl* paper is still made today, and in some regions of Mexico and Guatemala it is believed to be sacred and is used for magical purposes.

Unfortunately, the Indian "books," the records of their pre-Hispanic history, literature and arts, all but vanished. Fearful that the strange writings of the Aztecs and Mayas were works of the devil, the Spanish clergy and laymen systematically destroyed them. The handful that were saved, often sent to Europe as souvenirs were either lost or forgotten. In less than a generation after the conquest the descendants of the Aztecs and the Maya had lost the ability to read and write their native script.

By the eighteenth century cultured Spaniards living in Mexico and Central America had actually forgotten that imposing civilizations had existed in these lands years before the birth of Christ. In the United States and Europe people were equally unaware. The Scottish historian, Dr. William Robertson, who was as well known in his time as Arnold Toynbee is today, was positive that there had been no ancient people on the American continent capable of achieving any kind of civilization. In his *History of America*, he discredited the accounts of the Spanish conquistadors as so many pipe dreams. He wrote: "The Indian temples were merely mounds of earth covered with shrubs, without steps or facings of cut stone. There is not, in all that vast expanse, a single monument or vestige of any building more ancient than the conquest." He might have added, How could such people write?

For one moment, however, a ray of light shone upon the forgotten Mexican codices. In 1735 Lorenzo Boturini Benaduci went to Mexico to settle some business affairs for the Spanish Countess of Santibáñez. Having settled the Countess' affairs, and being a most religious man, Boturini began gathering data related to the miraculous nature of the Virgin of Guadalupe, Mexico's national patroness who had, according to legend, appeared before a humble Indian in 1551. He thought the miracle might have been depicted in the postconquest pictographic codices. Though he found no such record, the codices intrigued him and he began collecting them. He learned several Indian languages, and for eight years he scoured Mexico, gathering fragments of the "books." By 1743 he had an interesting collection which he called "my museum."

For some unknown reason Boturini aroused the suspicion of the Spanish viceroy. All but a few of his codices were confiscated and he was expelled from Mexico. On the voyage to Spain his hard luck persisted; his ship was captured by English pirates and his remaining treasures were taken as booty.

More than fifty years would pass before anyone again showed

an interest in the Indian writing and the forgotten American civilizations. The next investigator, the rediscoverer of the Americas, was Baron Alexander von Humboldt, one of the nineteenth century's few universal geniuses. With the exception of Napoleon I, Humboldt was probably the most famous man in Europe.

Humboldt was born in Berlin, September 14, 1769, the son of a major in the Prussian army. In his lifetime he distinguished himself as a geologist, naturalist, astronomer, geographer, philosopher, botanist, artist, linguist, diplomat and explorer. Every learned institute in Europe and the Americas tried to enroll him as a member. Kings and emperors—of Russia, Prussia, France, England and Austria—called upon him for advice and counsel. Bolivar, the leader of the South American liberation movement, called him the "second Columbus, the rediscoverer of the Americas."

Already a celebrity in his own country, in 1799 Humboldt set out to measure the Americas in a way no one else had ever done. For five years he traveled through much of South America and Mexico, even stopping in the United States to chat with Thomas Jefferson. During these years he filled and sent back to Germany more than fifty barrels and trunks of minerals, botanical specimens, sketches of pre-Hispanic monuments, scientific measurements and other observations. He explored the Amazon and the Orinoco rivers, climbed several of South America's highest peaks, discovered and studied volcanic fault lines, examined all kinds of archives and had time to learn several native American languages, including Peruvian Quechua and the Nahuatl of the Aztecs.

He became interested in the writing of the pre-Hispanic Indians when he came upon a sixteenth-century Peruvian manuscript written in Latin letters but in a native tongue. He sent the manuscript to his brother, Wilhelm von Humboldt, a well-known philologist in Germany. By the time he had reached Mexico, in 1803, he was eagerly tracking down every sample of the writing he called "hieroglyphics," hoping these would help him in the investigation of the origins of the Indians in the Americas. His most important manuscript discovery occurred while attending an auction in Mexico City where he purchased sixteen fragments of Indian codices. These were what was left of poor Boturini's "museum" which had been stowed away in a damp basement of the viceregal palace where flood waters and humidity had ruined most of the documents.

Although Humboldt devoted a great deal of time in tracking down examples of the ancient Mexican writing, he was never able to decipher it. Like Peter Martyr he saw a certain resemblance between it and the Egyptian hieroglphics and Chinese characters, but he realized these were only superficial. He sensed a closer relationship between the pictorial records of the Huron and Iroquois Indians in North America and the pictographs in the Aztec books. He felt that the system of the latter was far more advanced.

To a man of his brilliance it was obvious that the Mexican pictographs were not an alphabetic or a syllabic script—there were far too many signs. Yet he felt that some of the signs were more than pictorial representations of things, people and actions. He thought that some of these might be ideographs capable of recording abstract ideas. His research led him to surmise that the ancient codices contained a wide range of subjects: calendric records, mythological, astrological and magical formulae, and historical records.

When he returned to Europe, Humboldt continued his quest of Mexican documents. He combed through dozens of libraries— the Vatican, Florence, Oxford and the Archives of the Indies in Seville—where he found more fragments of codices than he had found in Mexico and Central America. In 1810 he published a two-volume report on American documents, devoting a large part of this work to pre-Columbian scrolls, their locations and condition. At the end of this work he said, "Notwithstanding the extreme imperfection of the hieroglyphic writing of the Mexicans, their paintings were good substitutes for books, manuscripts, and alphabetic characters."

Humboldt realized that in order to decipher an unknown script numerous texts should be assembled. He suggested that some institution, preferably one receiving government assistance, should track down all the existing Mexican codices. These should be published in color facsimile and distributed to scholars throughout the world. Although no government seemed willing to subsidize so monumental a project, a somewhat wild Irish nobleman decided to do so.

Edward King, Viscount of Kingsborough and eldest son of the Earl of Kingston, hardly seemed the man to devote his life to Mexican books. When he entered Exeter College at Oxford in 1814, he showed little aptitude for scholarship. He took no degree. Nevertheless, while at Oxford he fell under the spell of the colorful codices, little realizing that they would be his ruination.

His first contact with the Indian picture books, apart from his familiarity with Humboldt's work, was through a postconquest document on view at the Bodleian Library. It was called the Selden or Mendoza Codex, and had been compiled by Aztec scribes at the order of the first Spanish viceroy in Mexico, Antonio de Mendoza. In a certain sense it was a bilingual, containing Indian pictographs describing Aztec customs, a list of tributes rendered to Moctezuma and a Spanish commentary. The story of how this rare manuscript reached Oxford is interesting. Mendoza had dispatched it to Spain, but before it reached that shore French pirates seized it. They sold it to a Parisian antiquarian. It then passed through several hands before an Englishman, John Selden, purchased it and donated it to the Bodleian Library in 1664. It was lost in the stacks for 150 years and was only brought to light when Kingsborough was a student at Oxford.

At about the same time, other Mexican manuscripts began to pop up at the Bodleian. There was the Codex Laud, donated to the university by the book-burning Bishop of Canterbury, William Laud; there was another Selden-donated manuscript called the Selden Roll; and the still older Codex Bodley. Intrigued by these manuscripts and by Humboldt's suggestion that others like them be rescued from oblivion, young Kingsborough began reading everything available about the Spanish conquest of Mexico.

He must have realized that he could not afford to undertake the Humboldt project because, after leaving Oxford, he tried a political career. He was elected to Parliament as a representative from County Cork. But during these years he was haunted by the Mexican picture books; nothing would do but to devote all his time to the quest. Finally, in 1826, during his second term, he resigned his parliamentary seat in favor of his younger brother.

The thirty-year-old Kingsborough now began scouring museums and libraries from Spain to Hungary. He persuaded friends who were traveling in Europe to join in the search. When he could not purchase the codices or fragments of manuscripts he had uncovered, he employed a skilled draftsman, Agostino Aglio,* to make perfect copies. Five years were spent simply copying codices which had been located in libraries and museums. To supplement

---

* Agostino Aglio also traveled in Egypt with Giovanni Battista Belzoni and did the illustrations for Belzoni's book, *Narrative of the Operations and Recent Discoveries within the Pyramids, Temples and Excavations in Egypt and Nubia.*

the work of draftsman Aglio, Kingsborough sent an adventurer-artist, Jean Frederic Maximilian, Comte de Waldeck, to Mexico and Central America. Waldeck, in his youth, had accompanied Napoleon's expedition to Egypt. While Waldeck was sketching in America and Aglio was making facsimiles in Europe, Kingsborough himself was studying his growing collection of codices and writing copious notes for his grandiose project. He hunted down and translated numerous sixteenth-century accounts of life in Mexico. Among these was the manuscript of Fray Bernardino de Sahagun, an unusually important work about Indian Mexico. It had been lost for three centuries.

Obsessed by his project, Kingsborough thought in monumental terms—and damn the expense! He planned to publish a ten-volume work which would be called *Antiquities of Mexico*. In 1831 he published the first seven volumes. And what books! Each huge volume was printed in imperial folio (the largest book-page size): two copies of each were done on fine parchment, one for the British Museum, the other a gift to the Bodleian Library. Nine other sets were printed on special drawing paper and presented to the crowned heads of Europe. Still another special edition containing hand-colored prints was put on sale for £210 per set. The ordinary edition was offered at 140 British pounds the set. When the books appeared they caused a sensation, but unfortunately, very few people wanted to spend that much money for books about a distant, hardly known country. The price of the books soon fell to less than a quarter of what it had cost to print them.

Although volumes eight and nine were ready for publication, Kingsborough could not pay for the printing. He owed everyone: printers, illustrators, papermakers, binders, tailors, servants and grocers. His wealthy father, the Earl, refused to help him. Moneylenders and creditors howled for payment; they didn't care if Kingsborough was a member of the nobility, or that he would eventually come into a comfortable fortune when he inherited the earldom. Three times during this bleak period in his life he was thrown into the sheriff's prison in Dublin, and none of his family would come to his assistance. They believed he was mad. Anyone who had spent over £32,000 to print a few books must, indeed, be mad. During his last term in prison he came down with typhus and died, November 1837.

After his death the eighth and ninth volumes of his book were finally printed. The tenth volume of this magnificent and tragic obsession was never completed.

Kingsborough never tried, nor was he equipped, to decipher the curious glyphs and pictographs in the marvelous manuscripts to which he had devoted his life. He had developed farfetched theories about the pre-Hispanic Indians, including a belief that the Indian languages were Semitic in origin. Despite all this, his real contribution to the rediscovery of the American past and its languages was his recovery of many lost codices. In an oblique way, even after his death, he guided a young American traveler who would soon rediscover the world of the Maya and their script—which was more advanced and more puzzling than that of the Aztecs.

14

The Maya Riddle

One afternoon in 1836, a young American lawyer named John Lloyd Stephens called at the London home of Frederick Catherwood, a talented English illustrator. Over glasses of sherry the two men shared their impressions of Egypt, Palestine and Greece. Stephens had just completed a two-year tour of the Near East; Catherwood had traveled there a few years before. The American was excited by the antiquities he had seen. At one point Catherwood interrupted him, saying, "Would it surprise you that there might be similar ruins in your Americas?"

"It would, indeed," Stephens replied, amused.

"Then you should see Kingsborough."

"Kingsborough? What has he to do with America?"

"It might amuse you," Catherwood went on. "Kingsborough may be slightly daft you know. For years he's been collecting every document he can find concerning Mexico's pre-Columbian past. He is positive a high civilization once existed there. He

intends to prove that your American Indians are remnants of the Lost Tribes of Israel."

Although Stephens smiled with polite reserve, he did look into the matter. He was unable to meet Viscount Kingsborough because that unfortunate man was again in debtor's prison, but he spent hours at the British Museum admiring the magnificent parchment edition of Kingsborough's *Antiquities*. He was especially fascinated by the colorful facsimile of a codex which had been copied at the Royal Museum in Dresden. Its flamboyant art, its surfaces covered with incomprehensible glyphs, seemed quite different from the other codices in Kingsborough's collection.

Stephens did not realize, of course, that he was examining the most noteworthy of pre-Columbian codices. It was also the only example of Maya writing to be found in Europe at that time, though no one knew it was Maya.

Stephens returned to New York to resume his law practice. For a short while he was busy supporting his friend Martin Van Buren in a presidential campaign, but none of this seemed as interesting as the Mexico Kingsborough's books had revealed to him. Like the Irish nobleman, he began reading about the Spanish conquest and early settlement of that region. One day he came upon a dry military report made by a Colonel Galindo of Honduras; it mentioned an ancient ruined city in the jungle near the Copán River.

Stephens decided it search for it. When his friends ridiculed the foolhardy idea and brought out Dr. William Robertson's *History of America* to prove there were no such cities, Stephens merely replied, "I shall see, once and for all, whether the rumors about hidden cities down there are true or not."

In October 1839, Stephens and his English friend, Catherwood, sailed from New York for Central America. Stephens carried

146

with him very official-looking credentials; President Van Buren had named him a kind of roving ambassador to whatever Central American country he might visit. This was hardly the right equipment for two inexperienced explorers. The regions south of Mexico were fraught with danger. The jungle and mountain areas were unmapped. The countries were torn by civil anarchy. Bands of lawless men were burning villages and murdering the inhabitants.

As they traveled into Honduras the two young men were not spared close calls: they were shot at; some of their gear was stolen; once they were arrested by a band of soldiers who could not read their credentials, and who wanted to execute them. But they managed to survive and to reach their objective—a mysterious, ruined city almost crushed by jungle verdure. Not knowing its original name, Stephens named it Copán, after the river and a nearby village.

"The city was desolate," Stephen noted in his journal. "It lay like a shattered bark in the midst of the ocean, her masts gone, her name effaced, her crew perished, and none to tell whence she came, to whom she belonged, how long her voyage, or what caused her destruction—her lost people to be traced only by some fancied resemblance in the construction of the vessel, and, perhaps, never to be known at all."

Stephens hired some men from the nearby hamlet to clear the jungle tangle so he could measure the ruined buildings and monuments, and so Catherwood could sketch. They had scarcely begun when their project was threatened. A mestizo from the village claimed that the lost city was on his land; the foreigners were intruders. This complication was finally resolved after a good deal of negotiating. Stephens bought the entire city for fifty dollars. He thought the price was rather steep. Little did he know that today, to supply American and European collectors, illegal looters receive thousands of dollars for a single piece of sculpture or stela robbed from this and other ancient cities.

The work went on. As the brush was cut away, Stephens realized that Copán was no ordinary city. It was an enormous shrine, a kind of holy city, a metropolis of monuments dedicated to unknown gods. The main group of buildings was set upon a terraced citadel covering more than twelve acres and rising to a height of 125 feet. And upon this platform was a great stepped pyramid. At the western base lay a plaza surrounded by smaller temples made of cut stone and deeply etched with countless hieroglyphlike signs.

While Stephens guided the work crew, made measurements and took notes, Catherwood had run into problems. During one of their first days at the ruins, Stephens found his friend standing ankle deep in jungle muck, sheets of sketch paper scattered around him. He had been trying to capture on paper the involved carvings on a tall stone monument or stela. These very pillars, with their carved ceremonial figures and inscribed hieroglyphs, would one day become valuable clues in deciphering Maya writing.

"They baffle me," Catherwood complained. "They are unlike anything I saw in Egypt, or anywhere else. They are meant to say something, but they're so mysterious they seem to defy my eye and my hand."

In the end, Catherwood's art conquered. After days of study and pondering, he began to reproduce the strange Maya designs with an exactitude that only a camera with sophisticated lenses and lighting could do. It is well that his pen caught them when he did because many of the inscriptions on these stelae have since been destroyed by weather and by looters. His drawings are the only remaining record of some Copán glyphs now being studied by decipherers.

148

Bishop Landa's "Maya alphabet" from the Madrid manuscript found by Abbé Brasseur.

Leaving Copán, the two travelers continued their adventurous journey, locating and visiting other deserted Maya cities in Guatemala, Yucatán and southern Mexico. On returning to New York in July 1840, Stephens wrote his *Incidents of Travel in Central America, Chiapas and Yucatán*. It was published in 1841 and was an immediate sensation. Its delightful style, colorful anecdotes, and Catherwood's illustrations, has made it an enduring travel classic.

John Lloyd Stephens' report and Frederick Catherwood's brilliant etching were like a bomb exploding in the world of scholarship. In their travels they had discovered a hidden skeleton in history's closet. Historians saw their carefully built theories about man's history—as they imagined it—quickly crumble. New concepts of history had to be constructed. Although many scholars reluctantly admitted the existence of the long-ignored ruined cities, a stormy controversy raged in the United States and Europe. Room had to be made for an unsuspected American civilization.

Neither man made any attempt to read the strange glyphs they had found, but Stephens directed the attention of scholars by pointing out the similarity between the Maya signs in the Dresden Codex and the numerous glyphs found on stelae and temples in Middle America. He felt they were not decorative adornments but were, rather, linguistic signs. Also, because the same glyphs that he saw in Copán were again found several hundred miles to the north, at Palenque and in Yucatán, he stated boldly: "There is room for belief that the whole of this country [the Maya region] was once occupied by the same race, speaking the same tongue, or at least having the same written characters."

In this single deduction Stephens outlined the geographic size of the forgotten Maya world and suggested that it was an empire strongly united by language and a single culture.

But who were the Mayas? Who were the Aztecs? Where

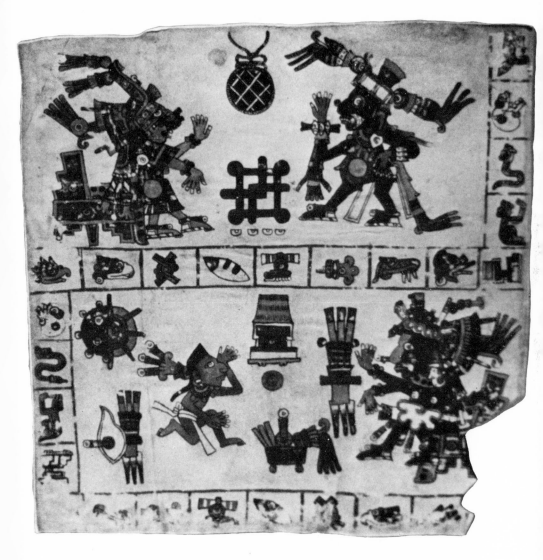

A segment of a pre-Hispanic Aztec codice (picture writing).
PHOTO: NORMAN, COURTESY, NATIONAL MUSEUM OF
ANTHROPOLOGY, MEXICO

had they come from? What was their history? What kind of civilizations had they created? No one seemed to know much about them. Even Stephens and Catherwood, who had been there, had no answers.

It remained for a blind explorer, who seldom left his darkened New England study, to provide a rich tapestry of these exotic cultures and to speed the development of New World archaeology and linguistic studies. An accident set this man, William H. Prescott of Salem, Massachusetts, on his career. Prescott had been studying law at Harvard, but one day while he was crossing the Boston Commons a crust of bread thrown by an exuberant student blinded him. Feeling that blindness would be a handicap in the courtroom, he gave up law and turned his energies to writing history books. He soon established a reputation with a work about Spain's Ferdinand and Isabella. Then he began a huge project—a broad history of the Spanish conquests in the Americas.

But how does a blind man dig in archives, read scarcely legible manuscripts or even write a book? The Braille system, typewriters and tape recorders had not been invented. Prescott developed an unusual system of working. He hired scholarly assistants to comb through the libraries of Europe, especially Spain. They sent copies of their research to Prescott's home in Boston. Meanwhile, in his darkened study, he used a simple apparatus called a noctograph to organize his notes. This appartus resembled a student's slate, but in place of the usual ruled lines there were brass ridges to guide his hand as he wrote. Friends read the material that was coming in from Europe, and Prescott jotted down what he needed. When he had made the notes he desired, they were read back to him repeatedly until he had memorized them. He became so proficient at this that he could hold sixty pages of printed material in his memory.

In 1843 his book *The Conquest of Mexico* was published. It was well received because never before had such a complete collection of original sources of information about the Aztecs and Mayas been brought together. He created a rich and vivid picture of the Indian societies, their folklore, their gods, their customs and their accomplishments. Prescott noted that these people had developed systems of writing, a sign of an advanced civilization.

He compared the Maya and Aztec forms of writing, pointing out that the Maya system did not appear to be as refined as the Egyptian hieroglyphics, but it was more advanced than the Aztec forms: "The writing shows an advanced stage of the art . . . and though somewhat clumsy, it is symbolical, and perhaps phonetic in character." Isolating the curious code of bars and dots which appeared in the Dresden Codex and on monuments from Copán to Palenque, blind Prescott made a remarkable surmise. "Possibly these dots denote years," he said. He had correctly identified the system of numbers by which the pre-Hispanic Mayas made their intricate calculations and dated their buildings and monuments.

1	6	11	16
2	7	12	17
3	8	13	18
4	9	14	19
5	10	15	20 or 20

Zero =

Although the Boston scholar had uncovered many valuable clues leading to the identity of the Maya people, he gloomily wondered if anyone would ever penetrate the veil of mystery surrounding the lost civilization. "The race itself is unknown," he observed. "And it is not likely that another Rosetta Stone will be found to guide an American Champollion to the path of discovery."

No Maya Rosetta Stone? About twenty years after Prescott voiced this complaint, something that looked as though it might serve as a Rosetta Stone was discovered by an energetic Belgian priest, Abbé Charles Etienne Brasseur de Bourbourg. Unlike Champollion's inscribed stone slab, the American counterpart was a manuscript written by a Spanish book burner. Along with other manuscripts from Yucatán and Guatemala, it would provide a great deal of information about the ancient Maya civilization.

The Abbé's career is worth recounting for its many contributions to the recovery of New World civilizations.

Charles Brasseur was born in the village of Bourbourg near Dunkirk in 1814. As a boy he was fascinated by the archaeological discoveries that had been made in Egypt, and by Champollion's decipherment of the hieroglyphics. Just as young Englishmen enlisted in the East Indian Company to further their careers, young men in France at this time entered the Church for similar reasons. To advance his education, Brasseur studied for the priesthood in Rome. After he was ordained he was sent to Quebec, Canada, where he taught Church history. Then from 1848 to 1851 he traveled as a missionary in Mexico and Central America, where he became interested in the pre-Columbian cultures.

He returned to Europe for two years (1851–1853) in order to do research in archives and libraries. During this time, while not engaged in religious duties, he supported himself by writing popular romances which appeared under the pen name of Etienne-Charles de Ravensberg. He returned to Mexico once more, and, for ten years, he wandered from north to south hunting down ancient manuscripts. During this time he learned a half-dozen native languages and made a number of important discoveries. His first valuable find was of a codex called *The Annals of Cuauhtitlán*, which has become a chief source of pre-Columbian history related to the inhabitants of the Valley of Mexico—the Toltecs, the Chichimecas and the Aztecs.

In 1855, while traveling in Guatemala, he found the famous *Popol Vuh* ("Book of the Community"), an unusually rich work of pre-Hispanic Indian literature.* It was a kind of national scripture relating the cultural history of the Maya-Quiche people up to 1550 A.D. Filled with legends, stories of migration, folklore, it has become a primary source for Maya myths and divinities. It had probably been transcribed from an ancient lost version into the sixteenth-century Mayan-Quiche tongue and written in Roman letters. It was kept hidden by the Indians until about 1700 when a Spanish monk, Fray Francisco Ximénez, was allowed to make a Spanish translation.

During his various search tours in Mexico and Guatemala the Abbé recovered other valuable works, among them *The Annals of Cakchiquels*, an historical work done at the time of the conquest. It was written in the dialect of the Maya-Cakchiquel Indians. He also found the *Motul Dictionary*, a Maya-Spanish dictionary compiled around 1550 by a friar at the Franciscan monastery in Motul, Yucatán. Later, in Madrid, he discovered another codice that is now called the Codex Troano.

Brasseur returned to Europe where he prepared and published

---

* Sylvanus G. Morley, the prominent Maya scholar, has made an excellent English translation of the *Popol Vuh*. The original Ximénez version of this document may be seen at the Newberry Library, Chicago.

his four-volume *History of the Civilized Nations of Mexico and Central America, During the Centuries before Columbus.* He also began issuing a series of documents in the Indian languages which he felt would further the study of the philology of ancient America.

By now Abbé Brasseur was being acclaimed by scholars and had been honored by the French government, but he was not ready to sit back and enjoy his laurels. He believed that the curious Maya glyphs were not just pictographs but might be a phonetic script. Dreaming of becoming another Champollion, he continued hunting for more codices and ancient manuscripts. Thus, in 1863, while digging in the musty archives of the Royal Academy of History in Madrid, his attention was caught by a Spanish document which appeared to be a Rosetta key to Maya writing.

The manuscript was entitled *Relación de las cosas de Yucatán* ("Report of Yucatecan Events"). It had been written in 1556 by Don Diego de Landa, archibishop of Yucatán. For almost three centuries it had been buried in the archives of the Royal Academy.

The Landa story is a strange one. Don Diego de Landa was an overzealous priest, so fired by his faith he was willing to destroy anything that seemed to threaten it. Yet, he also became the chronicler to the Mayas, preserving much of their history and ways. In 1549, shortly after the Spanish conquest of Yucatán, the young Franciscan friar, Landa, was sent to the peninsula and was stationed at the imposing monastery of Izamal. Eager to destroy the false gods and beliefs of the native Mayas, he carried on bitter campaigns.

One day word reached him that there existed a great Maya library hidden in the town of Mani which was one of the last centers of Maya-Itza culture in the region. Driven by an implacable fanaticism, he marched into Mani, holding a crucifix high before him. He ordered the mass imprisonment of the native nobles and had others tortured for their heathenism. On July 12, 1562, he staged an auto-da-fé in which a number of Maya leaders were burned and their native books destroyed by fire.

Even though Landa could not read the books, he claimed that they "contained nothing in which there was not to be seen superstition and lies of the devil."

Landa may not have burned all the Maya books. Nevertheless, the auto-da-fé and the book destruction was a cultural catastrope. Other churchmen in the New World condemned Landa's zeal, and he was sent back to Spain to stand trial before a court of the Council of the Indies. While awaiting the trial he wrote his *Relación*, perhaps as a defense and justification of his harsh treatment of the Indians. Whatever his intention was in writing it, the book has served anthropologists as a valuable source of information about the Mayas in Yucatán.

When Abbé Brasseur first uncovered the Landa manuscript he believed he had found the key to the Maya hieroglyphics. Landa gave a complete list of twenty-nine Maya glyphs which he called their alphabet, and he presented the corresponding Spanish vocal values. Scholars, however, could not make much sense of Landa's Maya alphabet or his interpretations of the Indian language. For more than a half-century the rediscovered work was rejected, but in recent years scholars and decipherers have begun to look at the zealous friar's interpretations in a different light.

15

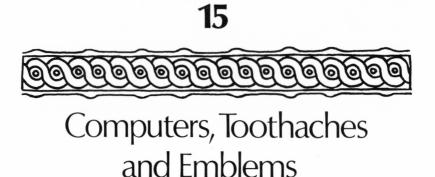

Computers, Toothaches and Emblems

The task of deciphering the pictograph and glyph writings of the Mexican and Central American civilizations has produced no single Champollion who could shout, "I have it." The decipherments which have been achieved, and not always with complete success, have resulted from persistent study, endless comparisons and fortunate insights, made by dozens of men and women —linguists, archaeologists, historians, artists, explorers and mathematicians. The recovery of the history, the arts, the beliefs and the legends of these ancient societies has been far more successful than the solution of their writing systems.

The symbolism and the meanings in the Mexican* picture-writing have been very well interpreted by modern scholars due to several factors: (1) There was close contact between the

---

* The terms *Mexican codices, Mexican writing* and *Mexican glyphs* are used in this chapter to identify the writing system of the Indians of central Mexico (Aztec, Toltec, Zapotec) as opposed to the Maya forms.

flourishing Aztec civilization and sixteenth-century Spanish chroniclers; (2) Mexican codices are more plentiful than the Maya; (3) A number of Mexican codices were made after the conquest; some of these bore Spanish or Latin explanations, thus serving as a kind of bilingual; and (4) The Spanish used native glyphs to communicate with the Indians.

For a short while after the conquest of central Mexico the Spanish authorities and missionaries made use of native pictographs and glyphs to inform the Indians of the new laws and beliefs they were expected to observe. The rebus principle was utilized. A picturesque example of this system, a rebus of the Lord's Prayer, is preserved in Mexico's National Library. Although Aztec speech had no provisions for such Spanish sounds as *f, g, r, d, b, s* and *j*, the Spaniards rendered the Latin *Pater Noster* with the following Aztec glyphs:

| pami-tl | te-tl | noč-tli | te-tl | Phonetic value |
| (banner) | (stone) | (cactus-pear) | (stone) | Pictograph meaning |

(COURTESY BIBLIOTECA NACIONAL DE MEXICO)

In speech the suffixes *tl* and *tli* were dropped and only the first sound of the object's name was pronounced. It produced the approximate Latin sounds for *pa-te noč-te* (*Pater Noster*).

Although recognition of the Mexican signs as a form of writing began with Kingsborough and Humboldt, not much progress was made in their decipherment until the 1890s because no one was able to develop a concept of the writing system, that is, an understanding of its structure or grammar so it might be read word for word. Gradually the reason for this failure became apparent. The

A detail of Maya glyphs carved on a stone lintel at Yaxchilán about A.D. 772. PHOTO: NORMAN

Mexican writing was neither a syllabary nor an alphabet with a fixed number of signs. Instead there were endless signs, a new one for almost every idea or object depicted. Some were pictographs, some were ideographs, and a few seemed to be phonetic. A decipherer could work out the meaning of one or more signs, but these failed to serve as clues to the sense of another text.

That scholars have been able to eke out the meanings from Mexican codices is one of the triumphs of American archaeology. No master key was available. Instead of using the usual tools of the decipherer—philological and etymological approaches, techniques of cryptanalysis—scholars have had to draw instead on the tremendous store of historical and anthropological material that fieldworkers and researchers have gathered over the centuries.

Bit by bit, over the years, students of Mexican picture writing have fitted small pieces into the gigantic picture puzzle. In the 1830s a French physicist, J. M. Aubin, who lost his scientific instruments while on an expedition in Mexico, passed the time by studying the codices. He was the first to recognize some of the rebus features in the writing system. At the turn of this century Charles Dibble, a leading student of the Aztec language, Nahuatl, discovered that the preconquest texts should be read from bottom to top, and the postconquest codices should usually be read from left to right. He also noted that as the Spanish influence increased, so did the rebus use of glyphs increase. Other Mexicanists such as Eduard Seler, the German botanist, Zelia Nuttall and Herbert J. Spinden, both American scholars, and Alfonso Caso, Mexico's present-day authority, have each made successful interpretations of the picture codices.

Thanks to their work, today we know that, to a great extent, the Mexican writing was not devised to be read word by word. The signs may have served as memory ticklers (mnemonic notations) for poems, songs, religious and historical works that were passed on by word of mouth from person to person and from generation to generation. The Aztecs, for example, maintained schools where young men were trained to memorize long passages of such folk literature.

Although the Mexican system sometimes seemed on the verge of evolving into a phonetic script, the hurdle was never fully cleared. The system remained basically a pictographic one in which cartoonlike figures, brilliant colors and even the position of figures in a codex were all meaningful. Many of the pictograms exhibited a delightful piquancy. The capture of a prisoner was indicated by showing someone being dragged by the hair; a series of footprints meant movement or walking; the conquest of a city was expressed by the picture of a burning temple. Most charming was the way in which speech was depicted: a tiny curlicue cloud issuing from the mouth of a figure meant "talking," if the curlicue was surrounded by flowers it indicated "singing."

*Musician beating tortoise
shell drum.*
(CODEX MAGLIABECCHI)

*Victory glyph, a temple
with a spear thrust into it
and flames curling skyward.*
(CODEX NUTTALL)

To express more abstract ideas pictographs and their name-sounds were combined as in rebus writing or puzzles. The Aztecs wrote the name of their capital, Tenochtitlán, by showing a nopal cactus, *noč-tli*, sprouting out of a stone, *te-tl*, then adding the suffix, *-an*, meaning "place."

*Aztec pictograph rebus for
Tenochtitlán (now Mexico City).*

Such combinations showed that the Aztecs had been on the brink of developing a phonetic script. In order to evolve a syllabary, the Aztec had only to fix, once and for all, a sign for a syllable, that is, the stone glyph for *te*, or the nopal glyph for *noč*, until they had as many signs as there were spoken syllables in their language. There are several reasons why this did not occur: first, the Spanish conquest ended the development of the native culture; second, the Aztec priest-scribes (the only people who were taught writing) attached a mystical power to the script and probably opposed any simplification of it; third, an alphabetic or syllabary script seldom develops in a short span of history. The Aztecs were around for hardly more than three hundred years.

Although the curious, fossillike script of the Aztecs still offers certain mysteries, it is the Maya glyph writing that presents the great challenge to twentieth-century decipherers. The system of the Maya was the most highly developed ancient writing in the Americas. Even though some of its signs appear distantly related to the Mexican signs, Maya remains an unknown language in an unknown script. For centuries men have attempted to crack its code, but the quest has been marked by false starts, controversial ideas about the language and, at best, plodding progress. Part of the difficulty is that there are only three known pre-Hispanic Maya codices and a number of stelae with glyph carvings scattered in museums around the world or buried in jungle ceremonial sites. Furthermore, the three codices (most accessible to scholars) date from 1300 to 1500 A.D., in other words, centuries after the decline of the classic Maya civilization. These few deal with religious augeries and calendric matters rather than with Maya history.

Attempts at Maya decipherments got off to a wrong start with Abbé Brasseur de Bourbourg. Despite his mastery of some modern Maya dialects spoken by descendants of the ancient Maya, and despite his recovery of many valuable documents, he failed miserably as a New World Champollion. He tried to solve the Maya puzzle by focusing on the etymology of Indian words. He decided there were fifteen thousand words in the Maya vocabulary, and he claimed at least half of these resembled the Greek of Homer. He also thought he could identify Indo-European roots in many other words, all of which led him to believe pre-Columbian America had been settled by Scandinavians.

The Landa manuscript which Abbé Brasseur uncovered seemed to offer scholars some directions. Although Landa's twenty-nine-character Maya alphabet confused Mayanists more than it helped them, the manuscript, at least, has assisted them in deducing the meanings of almost a third of the Maya glyphs. It is believed today, as far as the alphabet is concerned, that Landa may have been misinformed by the sixteenth-century Mayas; they may have simply made up sounds for the glyphs that they really couldn't read just to be accommodating; or, it is possible that the glyphs included in his manuscript may have represented sounds of the language spoken in Yucatán at the time of the conquest but were not related to the sounds and meanings of the ancient Maya tongue.

Maya stela at Yaxchilán. The dates carved in the stone coincide with our date, A.D. 772. PHOTO: NORMAN

Along with the *Popol Vuh*, other postconquest native documents shed some light on the Maya culture and its customs. The *Books of the Chilam Balam* (various versions from different Yucatecan towns) and *Annals of Cakchiquels* (a Maya people closely related to the Quiche) were written in sixteenth-century Maya dialects but using Latin letters which the authors had not mastered. In some manuscripts the words were strangely formed and run hopelessly together. Despite such obstacles, in 1882 the American scholar D. G. Brinton published brilliant English translations of the *Annals* and the *Chilam Balam of Tizimin*. Such Indian manuscripts contained clues to a Maya system of reckoning time and dating events which set decipherers off on a narrow but productive avenue of research—Maya numeration and time counts.

Prescott had already suggested that the dots and bars in the Dresden Codex might be numbers. Abbé Brasseur, despite his other errors, did some useful work in disentangling this numerical system. Then, five years after the publication of Brinton's translations, a German librarian named Ernest Forstemann, working with the Dresden Codex, deciphered some of the Maya calendar as well as their calculations of the movement of the planet Venus. At about the same time, Joseph T. Goodman, a Nevada mining tycoon and employer of a young journalist named Mark Twain, worked out the principle of Maya dating. His work was further refined and amplified by M. Hernández and the explorer-scholar Sylvanus G. Morley.

They revealed that the Maya system of counting was vigesimal, that is, based on multiples of twenty, much as our decimal system is based on tens. It was both simple and manageable. A dot was the equivalent of 1, a bar equaled 5, four bars (one above the other) stood for 20. The value of a numerical symbol depended on its position, just as our numeral 2 may have the value of 200 when it stands in the first position in the sequence 252, or it has the value of 2 when it is in the last position. Long before the time of Christ, the Maya were using a shell symbol to represent the abstract zero, a mathematical concept Europeans picked up from the Arabs during the Middle Ages. Numerals above 19 were indicated by dots, bars and shells. Calculations running into hundreds and thousands still used the shells, dots and bars, but the size of the figure depended on their positions in vertical columns.

8,000 line		$7 \times 8,000 = 56,000$
400 line		0
20 line	$11 \times 20 = 220$	$15 \times 20 = 300$
1st line	$8 \times 1 = 8$	$2 \times 1 = 2$
Totals:	$220 + 8 = 228$	$56,000 + 0 + 300 + 2 = 56,302$

The Maya used a vigesimal system based on 20. Unlike our decimal system in which the value of a digit depends on its position, reading from left to right, the Maya counted from bottom to top in multiples of 20.

Scholars discovered that the Maya calendar was as complicated as a Chinese puzzle; it resembled a series of wheels, one within the other, each revolving independently and recording interrelated cycles of time. One wheel was the *tzolkin* or religious calendar year of 260 days. Another was the *haab* or civil year made up of eighteen 20-day months, plus 5 nameless days, all totaling 365 days. While Europeans muddled along for centuries with the inaccurate Julian year, then shifted to the more refined Gregorian calendar, the Maya priests had, since the fourth century B.C., been using a system that comes much closer to the scientifically absolute year of 365.242,198 days. Their calendar year contained 365.242,129 days.

Since the Maya calendar was repeated every fifty-two years, rather than continuing indefinitely from a year-one, they utilized another reckoning method called the "long count" to mark how much time had elapsed from the beginning of their chronology. Their zero-date corresponds to about 3000 B.C. No one knows why this particular time was selected; it might have celebrated the birth of the Maya gods or the date of creation.

One of the most difficult tasks the Maya decipherers faced was to coordinate the Maya calendar with our Western calendar so that we could relate events in Maya history to the approximate times in our known history. This was done by comparing the astronomical observations and data recorded by ancient Maya astronomers with our own astronomical records. Furthermore monuments and stelae have been found bearing engraved Maya dates. Among the oldest dated monuments found in the Maya region are: a stela found by Sylvanus Morley with a date calculated to be April 9, A.D. 328, and the Leyden Plate, found in Guatemala, dated about A.D. 320. A far older stone with the dot-bar dating on it was found at Tres Zapotes, Veracruz; its confirmed date is 31 B.C. This calendric stone, however, is believed to have been carved by the Olmecs, a civilization older than the Maya. The Olmecs may have invented the Maya system of chronology. Many archaeologists believe they were the cultural innovators in Middle America and might be called the Sumerians of the New World.

Stela number 6 from Piedras Negras, Guatemala, showing either
a chieftain or a priest within a niche. The figure is framed by Maya
glyphs which include a calendar dating of A.D. 687.
PHOTO: NORMAN

Until the late 1940s most students of Maya writing felt that the glyphs were chiefly ideographic and required no knowledge of the ancient spoken language of the Maya to be understood. Thus, except for a few minor attempts to revive the phonetic approach, Maya studies focused on deciphering dates and calendric material. Inscriptions not related to this were usually ignored. But just as fashions in dress change, so do directions in scholarly inquiry change. In recent years scholars have turned their attention to the noncalendric glyphs and texts, looking at these once again from the viewpoints of the philologist, linguist and cryptanalysist.

A number of glyphs had already been deciphered; the signs for most of the Maya gods, for man, for rain, for animals, for drought and for many articles that the Maya used. Nevertheless, these seemed to be a drop in the bucket because there were approximately eight hundred individual glyphs recorded. But gradually advances in deciphering were made.

J. Eric S. Thompson, a noted contemporary Maya authority who has combined scholarly work with wide-ranging explorations in the Maya country, has found subtle grammatical forms in this "lost" language. He deciphered some of the puzzling affixes accompanying many of the glyphs. He determined that one of these, a curved bar with small dots along the edge, was a possessive sign; it was used by the ancient Maya and is still used in the modern Maya dialect of Yucatán. Thompson also detected some examples of rebus writing, but he saw no signs that the writing was syllabic in any way.

Between 1952 and 1963 a radical new approach was taken by a young Russian linguist, Yuri Knorosov. He proposed that the noncalendric glyphs were a mixed bag and that the signs might be better understood if they were viewed as phonetic syllables rather than as an alphabet. He argued that if Maya texts were simply composed of pictographs or ideographs the glyphs would occur with the same frequency throughout a long passage. In the texts he had examined, he found that the number of newly appearing signs diminished as the text progressed, an indication that he might be dealing with a number of recurring speech sounds. He suggested that certain pairs of glyphs had no symbolic or pictographic meaning in themselves, but were syllables in a phonetic system. Although Knorosov's approach has not been widely accepted by other Maya scholars, phonetic investigations continue.

The Guatemalan linguist, Otto Schumann, and several other students who speak a number of modern Maya dialects, are trying to re-create the old Maya tongue by searching for common elements in seven or eight dialects. Schumann reasons that if a certain word form or word sound is found in most of these dialects it is very likely to have been part of the original language. It is the same as if we were to study certain words that are common in Spanish, Portuguese, French and Italian in order to get a glimpse of the mother language, Latin.

In 1960 still another radical attempt at deciphering the Maya script was undertaken at the Mathematical Institute of the Russian Academy of Sciences at Novosibirsk (Siberia). Three young mathematicians, using Knorosov's material, set out to solve the Maya riddle with a modern weapon—the digital computer. Their idea was that the most frequent Maya glyphs would represent the most frequently used sounds in the ancient language. They felt they might relate the sounds in the modern Maya dialects, and sounds already identified from Maya texts that had been written in the alphabet of the Spaniards, to the most frequent recurring glyphs. They painstakingly codified sixty thousand glyph combinations on punch cards and memory drums. When everything was ready a button was pressed; the computer went to work in a forty-hour deciphering spree. Unfortunately, the results were not up to expectation, perhaps because the number of early codices used in the experiment and the range of modern Maya dialects used was too limited.

The computer method may eventually prove useful. Today, at Mexico's National University scholars are laboriously compiling a computer catalogue of Maya glyphs from the known codices, from carved stelae, temple carvings and pottery. Their object is to make a "map" of the texts so that decipherers might search for frequently used constructions and combinations, and in this way discover something about the grammatical structure of the glyph texts.

A similar group of dedicated searchers from several North American universities and museums is embarked on a million-dollar, fifteen-year project called the Maya Hieroglyphic Inscription Study. The purpose of the project is to assemble and catalogue by means of computers all the known Maya glyphs and texts existing in museums and libraries as well as inscriptions still lost in the jungles of Central America. The fieldwork for this Kingsborough-like operation is being directed by the Peabody Museum. At present, Ian Graham, an angular Scot, amateur archaeologist, explorer and photographer—a kind of latter-day Rawlinson or John Lloyd Stephens—has been ranging across Central America photographing the 1,322 inscriptions known to exist and searching for monuments and inscriptions still hidden in the jungles before they are destroyed by the elements or by looters.

New clues which may contribute considerably to the eventual solution and reading of the Maya script have been uncovered by two Mayanists who are neither professional linguists nor crypt-analysists. One of them is an artist connected with Harvard's Peabody Museum and the Carnegie Institution of Washington; the other is a Heinrich Schliemann-like merchant who retired from the wholesale grocery business to devote himself to Maya studies.

The artist is Russian-American Tatiana Proskouriakoff, Curator of Maya Art at the Peabody and archaeological research associate with the Carnegie Institute. Professor Proskouriakoff is noted for her magnificently detailed drawings and reconstructions of Maya architecture done while on expeditions in Yucatán, Guatemala and Honduras. While working with Maya inscriptions at the ancient ceremonial city of Piedras Negras in Guatemala, her attention was caught by the repetition of certain glyphs on a group of monuments related to a particular temple. The dates on these stelae revealed that they had been constructed at five-year intervals. Professor Proskouriakoff suddenly realized that the dates of a related group of monuments fell easily within the lifespan of a single individual. Was it possible that each group of stelae represented the reign of a single person? Did the carved figures depict rulers rather than gods and priests as was generally believed?

Professor Proskouriakoff made a careful study of thirty-five such monuments at Piedras Negras and continued her work at Yaxchilán and Naranjo, two important Maya cities of the classical period. An analysis of the glyphs on the stelae revealed that certain key signs seemed to relate to important stages in the ruler's life. In one group of monuments the first stela that had been erected depicted a young man seated in a niche. There were two glyphs shown with him: one, an upended frog glyph, recorded the birth date of the ruler; the second, called the "toothache" glyph (it looks like someone with a bandage extending from jaw to top of the head), or "accession" glyph, is believed to mark the young man's accession to the throne.

Maya glyphs interpreted by Tatiana Proskouriakoff.

"Upside-down frog"
glyph.

"Toothache" or
"Accession" glyph.

Monuments in this group which were constructed later show a woman and a child, indicating the ruler's marriage and birth of a son. Some of the accompanying glyphs have been identified as personal names and titles. It is not yet certain whether the dates on these monuments are purely historical. Because the Maya were both astronomers and astrologers, there is also the possibility that these dates may represent predictions of good and evil events in the ruler's reign.

Although Heinrich Berlin, the retired merchant who now lives in Mexico, worked in many of the same classic Maya cities, the clues he appears to have discovered have to do with place names. While examining and comparing Maya glyphs at Yaxchilán, Piedras Negras, Naranjo, Copán, Tikal and Palenque, Heinrich Berlin noted that certain glyphs seemed related to particular places. They are, in a sense, emblems peculiar to a site, much the same as the Eiffel Tower or Big Ben might identify Paris and London, or names such as Chicago, Tucson or Dallas are connected with a particular place and are used most often in those places. Since 1959 Berlin has isolated and identified a number of these so-called emblem glyphs.

Place or emblem glyphs, according to Heinrich Berlin.

Piedras Negras	Yaxchilán	Naranjo	Tikal

Even though these are rather limited discoveries many Maya scholars are convinced that the carved inscriptions found on temples and stelae in the ancient Maya cities may offer decipherers much more to work with than the late-period codices which deal primarily with calendric augeries and supernatural material. The carved inscriptions represent a period when the Maya civilization was at its height, and they seem to reflect the historical side of the culture. According to Maya scholar Michael Coe of Yale University, the inscriptions seem to be saying something about "the every day hurly burly politics of the Maya."

16

Pushing Back
Europe's Horizon

The decipherment of Egyptian hieroglyphics and Meso-
potamian cuneiforms reclaimed almost five thousand years of
written history about civilizations on the African and Asian side
of the Mediterranean, but it left Europe looking like a laggard
in the colorful tapestry of the past. Until the nineteenth century
most scholars believed that the earliest fullblown civilization, the
Hellenic, could only record its history to about 776 B.C.—the
symbolic date marking the first Olympic Games as well as the
adoption of the Phoenician alphabet by the Greeks. Any European history before that date was considered mythical.

But several unusual men changed this. They added more than
fifteen hundred years to Europe's known history; they scraped
away the crust of time from forgotten civilizations which had
developed their own systems of writing. None of these men were
professional linguists or philologists. One was a self-made mil-
lionaire merchant who believed in myths; the second was a well-

to-do English gentleman whose microscopic eyesight turned him into a world renowned archaeologist; the third was a brilliant British architect and wartime bomber-navigator who found the key to one of the most puzzling ancient scripts man has known.

Their story begins with myths. Although Greek history went back no further than the eighth century B.C., the Greeks had preserved many legends of a remote past, a hazy time when men performed heroic deeds and gods meddled in their affairs. The best known of the legends were embodied in the twin master-pieces of Greek literature: the *Iliad*, a long epic poem about a military expedition against Troy, and the *Odyssey*, a heroic account of Ulysses' return home from that war. Though these epics are attributed to the bard-poet Homer, who lived toward the end of the eighth century, they were certainly passed down by word of mouth for centuries before Homer gave them their epic shape.

In the *Iliad*, Homer tells how a Trojan prince, Paris, stole the beauteous Helen from her husband, Menelaus of Sparta and how Menelaus and his brother Agamemnon, king of kings, led a great expedition against Troy. After a long war they finally sacked the city, thanks to the stratagem of the Wooden Horse devised by wily Ulysses. Homer filled his tale with long lists of places from which the Greek forces came. Some of the places mentioned were: Agamemnon's proud citadel, "Mycenae, rich in gold", "wealthy Corinth and the good town Cleonae," and "men from Knossos, from Gortyn of the Great Walls, from Lyctus, chalky Lycastus, Phaestus, and Rhytion, fine cities all of them."

If you read the *Odyssey* you can trace the homeward journey of Ulysses the Wanderer, pinpointing his stops on any good map until he slips off of it into a world of fantasy. Many of the places Homer described are real and quite visible. "Out of the dark blue sea there lies a land called Krete, a rich and lovely land, washed by the waves on every side, densely populated and boasting ninety cities. One of these many towns is a great city called Knossos and there for nine years, King Minos ruled and enjoyed the friendship of almighty Zeus."

Yes, you can visit Crete, but you can't wander down to Hades with Ulysses. Nor do you quite believe that Helen was the daughter of the great god Zeus. You listen somewhat dubiously when Homer says that the superb warrior Achilles was the son of Thetis the sea nymph, or that his horse, Xanthus, spoke a human tongue. Most serious people during the nineteenth century looked upon these stories as delightful fairy tales or myths, but one romantic-minded German disagreed.

Heinrich Schliemann, born in Mecklenburg, Germany, January 6, 1822, believed in Homer. Since early childhood, when he first heard the stories about Troy, he was convinced he would find the mythical city. This seemed like a childish daydream because the Schliemanns had no money for travel or exploration. His father, an impoverished pastor who drank too much, could not even send his son to high school. At fourteen Heinrich was forced to become an apprentice grocer.

Nevertheless, driven by his dream, he spent an incredible life building a fortune and preparing himself to be the discoverer of ancient Troy. While gradually working his way up the businessman's ladder of success—grocer, accountant, cabin boy shipwrecked enroute to Venezuela, military contractor and independent merchant prince—he taught himself eight languages including Arabic and ancient and modern Greek. He amassed a fortune in Europe, then added to it as a banker in California during the gold rush where, incidentally, he became an American citizen.

At the age of forty-six he retired from business in order to pursue his dream. He went to Greece, married a Greek woman, and together they set out to search for Troy. Schliemann made some shrewd guesses. Reading his Homer carefully, he found the site of Troy on the coast of Asia Minor. Actually there was more than one Troy; there was a series of ancient cities, one buried beneath the other. During the difficult excavations the wealthy Schliemanns found more wealth—golden treasures, artifacts and implements such as Homer had described. The sensational discovery echoed through Europe. Homer was history, not myth.

Schliemann could have sat back to enjoy his sudden fame, but he was not through hunting with Homer. He turned his attention to the Greek mainland and searched for "Mycenae, rich in gold." Some people thought he was still treasure hunting, but in actuality he was searching for the grave of Agamemnon, who, on returning home from the Trojan War, had been treacherously murdered by his queen, Clytemnestra, and her lover, Aegisthus. He not only found what he was looking for, again proving that there was much historical truth in Homer, but his diggings accidentally led to the discovery of something equally important—that an advanced civilization had existed on European soil a thousand or more years before the Hellenic.

Schliemann did not fully realize this. He believed his findings were of the Homeric period rather than far older. But he had uncovered some puzzling objects never mentioned by Homer. Among these there was a bull's head of silver with two long golden horns, and "two other bull's heads of very thin gold plate which had double axes between the horns." He also dug up a large number of beautifully carved seals, some in the form of signet rings. Other archaeologists who had begun excavating Homeric sites on the mainland and on the Greek islands uncovered still more of these curious seals. Soon there was a great deal of debate concerning the makers of these artifacts. Obviously they came from an advanced culture. Who were its people? Where had they come from? Had they invented or borrowed a writing to record their history?

The person who came up with the answer to these questions was a young Englishman named Arthur Evans. In 1883, while on his first trip to Athens, he visited with Schliemann. Although he was not obsessed by the Homeric tales as was Schliemann, he was fascinated by the curious seals and signet stones the German showed him. The extremely fine and intricate carved stones in some way reminded him of Assyrian and Egyptian gems. They seemed far older and quite unlike the art of classical Greece. One of the reasons why these tiny glyphlike seals attracted him more than Schliemann's extensive archaeological excavations was his physical handicap. Evans was so nearsighted that any large object was a blur, but on the other hand, he saw small objects clearly. According to his half-sister, Joan, if he held a minute object before his eyes, "the details he saw with microscopic exactitude, undistracted by the outside world, had greater significance for him than for other men."

Although the tiny seals eventually determined Arthur Evans' career, he was not yet ready to let them obsess him. He had too many other interests. Unlike Schliemann, he had had the advantage of a good early education. Evans had been born in 1851 at Hemel Hempstead, England, to a well-to-do family. His father, a distinguished geologist and antiquarian, encouraged him in every way. Arthur won history prizes at Harrow, read history at Oxford, became expert in classical languages, collected ancient coins and studied art history. For a while, after leaving the university, he involved himself in the culture and the aspirations of the

Balkan people and so actively supported their independence movement that he was expelled from Ragusa in 1881.

After making a tour of Greece, where he visited Schliemann in 1883, he returned to Oxford and became the Keeper of the Ashmolean Museum. One day while examining some carnelian seal stones which had been donated to the museum, he noticed how similar they were to the seals Schliemann had shown him. He was further intrigued by the tiny carvings on them; they resembled a kind of hieroglyphic writing, a bit like Hittite signs he had recently seen.

Minoan seal from Crete

Now the seals set him off on a lifetime quest. He made another trip to Greece to collect similar seal stones and, while purchasing a large number of them from antique dealers in Athens, he was told each time that they had come from Crete. By 1893 he had collected enough of the seals, and had received impression copies from other European museums, that he formed a theory about them. At the end of the year he presented a paper to the Greek Archaeological Society in London, announcing that he had found sixty hieroglyph symbols on the seal stones. He believed they belonged to a pictographic script of Cretan origin. It was possible, he felt, that Crete, lying in the Aegean Sea halfway between Egypt and the Greek mainland, was an important stepping-stone between two worlds; perhaps the ancient people of Crete had developed an advanced culture and a written language.

A Minoan fresco of a young prince in the palace at Knossos, Crete.
PHOTO: NORMAN

The following spring he went to Crete. His diary records his exciting first day ashore:

> 1894, March 15, Heraklion: Arrived considerably worse for the voyage . . . twenty-four hours from Piraeus . . . The lion of St. Mark guards the harbor; Venetian walls defend the city and in the streets a few Venetian buildings, less splendid than those of Dalmatia, but still of the same type, rise side by side with Turkish fountains, plane trees and Turkish mosques . . . able to visit the bazaar; found Crysochoi, and a man from whom I bought 22 early Cretan stones for 1½ piastres each, two small Greek heads from Gortyna, some coins, one silver from Phaestos, and a small marble image from Phaestos . . .

He knew, indeed, this was Homer's "Krete of the ninety cities" —Knossos of King Minos, Gortyna, Phaistos and Lycastus; Crete where Zeus was born in a cave on Mount Ida and nourished by honey brought to him by bees.

As he explored Crete, to his surprise he found that the native women wore the cameolike seals he was collecting. The women prized them as amulets, calling them *galópetras* ("milkstones") in the belief that the charms produced milk when they suckled their infants. Thinking that he might find still more seals, perhaps even an engraved tablet with bilingual inscriptions which might provide a key to the ancient Cretan writing, Evans decided to dig at the site of legendary Knossos. The locale, a short distance from Heraklion, was shrouded with myths.

It was believed to be the marvelous capital of King Minos, son of the god Zeus. Beneath its palaces there was said to be a tremendous labyrinth created by Daedalus, the master craftsman. Within the labyrinth lived a terrifying monster called the Minotaur, to which Greek youths were sacrificed. Here, according to legend, Princess Ariadne provided the Greek hero Theseus with the precious thread that guided him safely out of the labyrinth after he had slain the beast.

Evans was not the first person to think of digging at the site. Schliemann had tried to purchase the property where Knossos was believed to be buried but had been unable to reach an agreement with the landowners. An American journalist, W. J. Stillman, and a Frenchman named Joubin had also tried to secure digging rights. A native of Heraklion, Minos Kalokairinos, had managed to sink five shafts in the area, establishing the fact that there seemed to be an enormous building deep beneath the earth. He had also uncovered a storeroom filled with a number of huge *pithoi*, that is, Ali Baba–style jars in which oil or grain had been stored.

Four years of dickering went by before Evans finally had title to the land. In March 1899, he began what he estimated would be a year of digging. Assisted by several associates and a large number of Cretan workmen, Evans soon began uncovering a great complex of buildings, some of them decorated with fragments of beautiful murals. His journal entry for March 27 reflected his excitement:

> Extraordinary phenomena—nothing Greek—nothing Roman—perhaps one single fragment of late black-varnished ware among the tens of thousands. Even Geometrical [7th century B.C.] pottery fails us, though as *tholoi* ["tombs"] found near the central road shows that a flourishing Knossos existed lower down . . . nay, its great period goes at least well back to the pre-Mycenaean period.

In a later letter to his father he wrote:

> The great discovery, is whole deposits, entire or fragmentary of clay tablets analogous to the Babylonian

but with inscriptions in the pre-historic inscription of Crete. I must have seven hundred pieces by now. It is extremely satisfactory. It is what I came to Crete seven years ago to find, and it is the coping stone of what I have already put together. These inscriptions engraved on the wet clay are evidently the work of practiced scribes, and there are also many figures no doubt representing numerals. A certain number of characters are pictographic, showing what the subject of the document was.

Evans' original intention was not to excavate Knossos completely, but merely to find sufficient seal stones and tablets in order to decipher the Cretan scripts. By now he had discovered three kinds of writing (later he was able to assign historical periods to their development). The earliest writing (2000–1650 B.C.) consisted of pictorial signs—heads, hands, stars, arrows— on seal stones and on a few clay tablets. He called these "hieroglyphics" since they resembed the early pictographic script of Egypt in style.

The next stage of writing (1650–1450 B.C.) seemed to have developed from the first, but the pictorial signs were simplified to mere outlines. Evans called this script, which ran from left to right, Linear A. A curious thing about this script is that numerous examples of it have been found all over Crete and on pottery on the islands of Thera and Melos but, thus far, nowhere else.

Minoan Linear A script from a clay tablet found in the small palace of Hagia Triada, Crete.

The Phaistos Disc from the Minoan civilization. The Linear A
script (pictographs) was stamped in wet clay, then sunbaked.
PHOTO: NORMAN, COURTESY HERAKLION MUSEUM

The third stage of writing, called Linear B, seemed to be a modified form of Linear A. No one is sure when this modification took place. Oddly, some four thousand Linear B tablets and fragments of tablets were found at Knossos but *nowhere else* on Crete. Vast numbers of Linear B tablets have been found, however, at various sites on the Greek mainland. The Linear A and Linear B forms of writing ceased to be used on Crete at about the same time, shortly after Knossos was destroyed (about 1450 B.C.), but Linear B writing was still in use on the Greek mainland for another two hundred years.

Although Arthur Evans had planned to dig for a season then settle down and decipher the Cretan script, before the summer of 1899 was over he abandoned decipherments in order to uncover a civilization.

For twenty-five years Evans continued excavating and reconstructing the palaces at Knossos. The story of his discovery of a forgotten civilization which he called "Minoan," after the legendary king, can only be mentioned briefly. The Evanses, father in England and Arthur on Crete, financed the exploration out of their own personal fortunes.

As the digging progressed, sometimes with more than two hundred men working, it became evident that Knossos had several palaces covering about six acres. The splendid architecture and engineering were such as only could be produced by a civilization of great age. Although the artifacts and decorations were somewhat similar to what Schliemann had found at Mycenae, the latter seemed to date back no earlier than about 1600 B.C., while findings at Knossos appeared far older. Test shafts revealed that there had been human settlements at Knossos continuously from the Neolithic Era, which ended about 3000 B.C.

Gradually putting together evidence collected at Knossos, and

West portico of the palace at Knossos, restored in part by Sir Arthur Evans. PHOTO: NORMAN

by fellow archaeologists working elsewhere on Crete, Evans divided Cretan history into three periods: Early Minoan (3000–2000 B.C.); Middle Minoan (2000–1600 B.C.); and Late Minoan (to about 1250 B.C.). How were these dates worked out? The answer is related to Minoan seamanship and Champollion's decipherment of Egyptian.

At the height of their civilization the Minoans became the first great naval power in the Aegean and the Mediterranean. Their ships carried Minoan trade goods, pottery, even seals, to the mainland of Greece and to Egypt. They brought back, in turn, Egyptian pottery and other objects. Since, thanks to Champollion, Egyptian history and the arts of each of its dynasties was well known, Arthur Evans was able to date the Egyptian artifacts buried at various levels at Knossos. Enough evidence was found to show that the Minoans were in contact with the Egyptians from around 3000 B.C., to around 1450 B.C.

But who were these people, the Mycenaeans and Minoans, that Schliemann and Evans had found? Where did they come from? Did they record their histories in their Linear A and Linear B scripts? And what were the decipherers doing?

In 1899 Arthur Evans published at Oxford his handsomely illustrated book *Scripta Minoa I*. It dealt chiefly with the pictographic glyphs he had discovered. In the foreword he announced the preparation of volumes two and three, which would deal with the two Linear scripts. In *Scripta Minoa I* he included a few examples of Linear A inscriptions that he had found at Knossos as well as fourteen examples of Linear B writing. Unfortunately, he kept putting off the publication of volumes two and three.

Despite Evans' tremendous contribution to Aegean archaeology, he delayed not merely his own decipherment of the inscrip-

Lineal B seal stones found at Knossos, Crete, by Sir Arthur Evans.
PHOTO: NORMAN, COURTESY HERAKLION MUSEUM

tions but also the possibility of other men deciphering the Minoan writings. In a sense, he hid the evidence. He was intensely possessive about Knossos, wanting no one to dig there or share in the cost of the operation. It was his. In the same way, he wanted the glory of deciphering the unusual scripts. Twenty-six years after *Scripta Minoa I* came out with its meager examples of the Linear scripts, he got around to publishing the fourth volume of his huge *Palace of Minos*, including in it only 120 reproductions of the 2,800 Linear B tablets that he had uncovered. Finally, eleven years after Evans died, his former pupil and fellow excavator, Sir John Myres, was permitted to publish the unfinished *Scripta Minoa II*, which contained the bulk of the Linear B illustrations.

Although he feuded bitterly with several noted scholars who, impatient at his delays in publishing his findings, attempted preliminary studies of the tablets and seals, Evans himself made only a few contributions to their decipherment. He managed to decipher the Minoan numerals. He recognized the small vertical strokes which served as word separators. He also sensed that the clay tablets he had collected were chiefly inventories, catalogues, lists of persons, animals and objects. To Evans, the Minoans seemed to be compulsive accountants.

Nevertheless, after two generations of delays, scholars finally had the opportunity to work on the scripts.

17

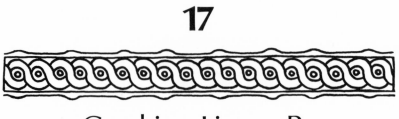

Cracking Linear B

Decipherers have not worked extensively with the early Minoan pictographs because too little material has been turned up, but the two Linear scripts posed real challenges. From the beginning of this century until about 1950 progress in solving either of the scripts moved at a snail's pace for several reasons: first, Sir Arthur Evans was reluctant to publish copies of the Linear B tablets he had collected; second, no Behistun Rock, Rosetta Stone or other bilingual of the scripts had been turned up; third, most scholars were thrown off target by a pet theory of Evans that neither of the Linear writings had anything to do with the Greek language.

Some initial attempts at solving the puzzles immediately limped up blind alleys. In 1931 F. G. Gordon published a book relating Minoan to the unique language of the Basque people living in the Pyrenees mountains at the other end of Europe. A little later Bedřich Hrozný, who had so brilliantly opened the way to reading Hittite cuneiforms, tried to prove that Linear B was related to Hittite and to the still unsolved Indus Valley script. (Hrozný may be excused for he was now quite old, feeble and, as one kind colleague said, "his mind is chock full of languages; naturally they get mixed up.") Another scholar, A. Cowley, came close to finding the key when he thought he recognized the Greek words for "boy" and "girl" in Linear B. He never went beyond this.

The picture began to change around 1939 when scholars received a windfall. A Greek-American expedition led by Dr. Carl W. Blegen of the University of Cincinnati and Dr. Constantine Kourouniotis of Athens located the ruins of a great Mycenaean palace near Pylos in western Messenia. It was the palace of King Nestor, a personage named in the third book of the *Odyssey*. During the excavation six hundred clay tablets were found, all in Linear B script. Although Dr. Blegen had to leave his Pylos tablets in the vaults of the Bank of Athens and return home at the outbreak of World War II, his assistant, Emmett L. Bennett, Jr., photographed and published them. Sir Arthur Evans' monopoly of Linear B samples was broken.

Even though the war delayed an immediate attack on the script, it served to train a number of men who would be involved in solving Linear B. Dr. Emmett Bennett, for example, became a U.S. Air Force cryptographer. After the war he became a leading authority on Mycenaean texts; in one of his published studies of the Linear scripts he noted something that had escaped most scholars. His code-breaking training showed him that though the graphic signs in Linear A and Linear B looked the same, the words were different. In short, there seemed to be two quite different languages using the same signs. It was like saying that though the same letters are used, English and Spanish are different languages.

Since there were far more examples of Linear B than of the other Minoan scripts, decipherers began to concentrate upon it. Between 1943 and 1950, Alice J. Kober, a brilliant young professor of Classical Studies at Brooklyn College, laid the first solid foundations for its decipherment. Although Dr. Kober once stated that she thought the Cretan scripts could not be unraveled, she did not let this deter her. The master of a formidable array of languages—Sanskrit, Hittite, Old Persian, Akkadian, Basque, Arabic, Hebrew and Greek—she applied her knowledge of their structures and differences to Linear B.

One of her first discoveries was that certain signs appeared over and over in certain positions of some written words. These changes were usually at the end of the word. This was an indication that Linear B was an inflected language. Languages having grammatical inflections usually change the form of the word by varying the ending to indicate differences in tense, gender, number of person. For example, the imperfect tense of the Spanish verb *to be* is inflected in the following manner:

era	I was	*éramos*	we were
eras	thou wast	*erais*	you were (plural)
era	he, she was	*eran*	they were

Modern English, though less inflected, makes similar changes. To indicate the plural of a noun we usually add an *s*; to show the past tense of a verb we add *ed*.

Although Dr. Kober still did not know the identity of the language she was untangling, she began to isolate a number of these inflectional signs and to determine the masculine and feminine forms. But tragically, just as she was on the verge of a decipherment breakthrough, this talented forty-three-year-old Brooklyn scholar died, on May 16, 1950.

Like members of a relay team, Doctors Kober, Blegen, Bennett and a few others had run the race this far. Now they passed the baton of the winning team to a young Englishman, Michael Ventris, who would cross the finish line.

In 1936 the British School of Archaeology at Athens celebrated its fiftieth anniversary with an exhibit at Burlington House in London. The speaker for the occasion was eighty-five-year-old Sir Arthur Evans. Michael Ventris sat in the audience, utterly enchanted by Sir Arthur's descriptions of Knossos. When Evans mentioned that the Cretan scripts were still undeciphered, fourteen-year-old Ventris vowed he would someday solve the baffling script. But unlike Champollion, who spent his entire youth preparing himself to meet the challenge of Egypt's hieroglyphics, Ventris did not even consider becoming a philologist.

The son of a comfortably situated family (his father was an army officer, his mother a gifted woman of Polish extraction), Ventris received a sound classical education. He showed some interest in languages. While studying in Switzerland, he mastered French, German and a Swiss dialect; at Stowe School in England he studied the Greek classics and, in his words, "I did a bit of Greek." Although he had also become proficient in Polish and Swedish, rather than continue through university he enrolled in the Architectural Association school in London.

During these years he had collected copies of the Linear B script, read everything he could on the subject and had begun corresponding with Alice Kober, Emmett Bennett, Carl Blegen and Bedřich Hrozný. World War II interrupted both his tinkering with Linear B as well as his architectural studies. Ventris' choice of military service reflected something of his character and the bent of his mind. He was, at this time, a handsome and charming young man, but unlike his fellow students who dreamed romantically of being daring fighter pilots in the Royal Air Force, Ventris joined the R.A.F. but elected to become a navigator in the Bomber Command. As he explained it, "the mathematical problems involved in navigating an aircraft seemed to offer more interest than being a driver."

At war's end he returned to architectural school and received his diploma with honors. By now the twenty-six-year-old Ventris' tremendous capacity for work, and his brillance, became apparent. He had that rare ability to divide his energies to the utmost. As an architect he had a capacity for infinite detail: his memory was photographic, his draftsmanship beautiful. His brain worked with astonishing rapidity, solving problems with the speed of a computer. Although he was unusually busy working on government architectural projects, he had time to picnic and party with his wife and two young children, and he had time left over for Linear B.

As he struggled with the Cretan scripts, exploring different approaches, he made copies of his work notes and circulated them among other scholars. During this period a flood of additional Linear B samples became available. Evans' *Scripta Minoa II* was finally published. Although it contained many errors (Evans had not been a good draftsman and had carelessly copied many of the signs), Dr. Emmett Bennett went to Crete to check the published copies against the original tablets. Meanwhile, Professor Blegen, digging again at Pylos in 1952, uncovered another four hundred Linear B tablets. Photographs of these, of course, were not yet available.

Despite the flood of new materials, experts gloomily predicted that Linear B could not be solved unless a useful bilingual was found. Ventris seemed to agree that the script would not yield to simple decoding; a more subtle system of deduction was needed.

"It is rather like doing a crossword puzzle on which the positions of the black squares have not been printed for you," he said.

He was already following four avenues of attack. First, as Evans had done, he analyzed the pictographic signs to determine the subjects listed on the tablets. Many of these were easy to identify—signs for grain, for olives, for chariots and for other material things.

Second, he made a statistical analysis of the way each sign was used, hoping to identify the kind of sound it might represent. He searched for signs that appeared frequently as an initial, believing they might offer a clue to initial sounds in some other known language of the period. Phoenician? Greek? Hittite?

Third, he pursued Alice Kober's lead, analyzing changes in the forms of words.

Fourth, he studied the context in which each separate word occurred in order to determine from its location whether it was a place name, a personal name or an ordinary vocabulary word. He hoped to find some words on the tablets which the Greeks may have borrowed from earlier inhabitants of the Aegean Islands, perhaps from the Minoans.

It was already known that the Linear B system of writing had about eighty individual signs, indicating it was probably a syllabary. Thus, instead of having one letter per sound as in an alphabetic system, there would be combinations. For example, in place of the letter *t*, there might be five or more signs for the syllables *ta, tu, to, te* and *ti*. Again taking a lead from Alice Kober, Ventris designed a homemade, nonelectronic computer— his famous syllabic grid—a large checkerboard divided into eighty squares with five vowel letters across the top and sixteen consonants down the side.

He drove nails into this board so that he could hang or move

Grid on which Michael Ventris advanced the phonetic values for 68 of the 88 signs of the Linear B script.

Consonant	Vowel 1	Vowel 2	Vowel 3	Vowel 4	Vowel 5
(H-)	A · AI	E	I	O	U
D-	DA	DE	DI	DO	DU
J-	JA	JE		JO	
K- G- CH-	KA	KE · KWE	KI	KO	KU
M-	MA	ME	MI	MO	
N-	NA · NWA?	NE · NEKO?	NI	NO	NU
P- B- PH-	PA	PE · PTE	PI	PO	PU
QU- GU-		QE	QI?	QO	
R- L-	RA · RJA	RE	RI	RO · RJO	RU
S-	SA	SE	SI	SO	SU
T- TH-	TA · TJA	TE	TI	TO	TU
W-	WA	WE	WI	WO	
Z-		ZE		ZO	ZU?

about tags with Linear B signs, until he found the right combinations. He described his system thus:

> The sign for *to*, for instance, is then put in the square where the *t* and the *o* intersect. The most important job in trying to decipher a syllabary from scratch, is to try to arrange the signs provisionally on a grid of this sort, even before we can work out the actual pronunciation of the different vowels and consonants. If we find evidence that two signs share the same consonant, like *ta* and *ti*, we fit them on the same horizontal lines. Once we can determine, later on, how only one or two signs were actually pronounced, we can immediately tell a good deal about many other signs which lie on the same columns of the grid.

He was aware that a great deal of information about the structure and grammar of an unknown language might be deduced from the way in which words were formed and changed. He felt that if he knew enough about the structure, then he could identify the language. Up to now, however, Europe and America's leading philologists were divided about the character of the Cretan scripts. Some were positive that the writings were related to Hittite dialects of Asia Minor, some thought there were connections with a primitive Anatolian language, others believe they might be related to the Cypriotic script which George Smith, of Gilgamesh fame, had deciphered in 1872. Dr. Alan J. Wace, who had been forced to give up the directorship of the British Archaeological Institute at Athens because he had disagreed with some of Arthur Evans' pet theories, suggested that the Mycenaeans might be of Greek stock. Might not Linear B, which they used for so long, be an archaic form of Greek using a Minoan syllabary?

Although Ventris did not believe Linear B could be Greek, continued work with his grid actually forced him to recognize certain Greek phonetic values in the signs. Reluctantly, he began to make out a few words which looked like and sounded like a truncated, archaic Greek. He still balked at accepting the idea. In his last work notes, No. 20, he said, "It is a frivolous digression." But it was not at all as wasteful of his time as he had imagined. As he continued to explore what the logic of his grid had forced on him, he began recovering more and more primitive forms of familiar Greek words such as *shepherd, goldsmith, bronzesmith* and *potter.*

Now he accepted the idea that Linear B might actually be a written form of the Greek tongue using Minoan signs. Although he recovered still more words and deciphered short lines of text, and he felt confident he had the key to the strange script, still he made no boastful claims. He felt he needed the help of someone who knew archaic Greek dialects. Such assistance came quickly. Sir John Myres put him in touch with a young Cambridge University philologist named John Chadwick. The latter was Ventris' kind of man. Chadwick was cheerful, energetic and the possessor of a keen mind. Chadwick not only knew several Oriental languages, including Tibetan, but he was an authority on ancient Greek dialects. What made their collaboration even more successful was that Chadwick was interested in Linear B, he had been reading some of Ventris' work notes, and he believed Ventris was on the right track.

The two young men worked together so well that before long, to amuse themselves, they wrote notes to each other in the Linear B script. Finally, having ironed out differences and come to agreement on most points, they issued a joint decipherment report which was printed in the 1953 issue of the *Journal of Hellenic*

Studies. A few years later it was amplified and published in book form and titled *Documents in Mycenaean Greek.* In both the report and the book they showed that the language of Linear B was indeed an ancient form of Greek. On first sight it seemed unlike known Greek because the tablets were a thousand years older than the language of Socrates. It was like the difference between the English of Beowulf and Shakespeare.

It was surprising that the normally cautious community of world scholars accepted Ventris' solution rather rapidly. One of the reasons for this swift accord was a startling letter Ventris received in May 1953 from Professor Blegen, who had been cleaning and photographing his new Pylos tablets. Ventris was so excited he immediately telephoned from London to Chadwick's Cambridge apartment. He excitedly read the letter, which ran:

> Since my return to Greece I have spent much time working on the tablets from Pylos . . . I have tried your experimental syllabary on some of them.
>
> Enclosed for your information is a copy of P641 [the tablet identification], which you may find interesting. It evidently deals with pots, some of three legs, some with four handles, some with three, and others without handles. The first word by your system seems to be *ti-ri-po-de* and it recurs twice as *ti-ri-po* (singular?). The four-handled pot is preceded by *qe-to-ro-we*, the three-handled by *ti-ro-we* or *ti-ri-jo-we*, the handle-less pot by *a-no-we*. All this seems to be too good to be true. Is coincidence excluded?

The Pylos tablet with its figures of tripods and pots became convincing proof that Ventris' ancient Greek Linear B syllabary was working. The young architect's decipherment of a language that had been spoken by the legendary heroes of the Trojan War was a landmark solution. One scholar connected with the British

Blegen's tripod tablet from Pylos which confirmed Ventris' decipherment.

Museum called it "the Everest of Greek Archaeology." It was truly a feat of pure reason and logic, a decipherment worked out without bilinguals, worked out almost entirely on the observable interrelationships of the script signs. Michael Ventris had pushed back the margins of the Greek language by some seven hundred years. From a distance of thirty-two centuries he had recovered the earliest form of a language that still lives.

Although Ventris was honored by his government, by universities and learned societies, he hardly lived long enough to enjoy the fruits of his achievement, for on the night of September 5, 1956, he met with a tragic accident. While driving home on the Great North Road near Hatfield, his car crashed into a truck and he died instantly.

Despite Michael Ventris' remarkable breakthrough, historians were disappointed when the Linear B tablets from Knossos, Mycenae and Pylos were translated. Unlike the hieroglyphics of Egypt or the Mesopotamian cuneiforms which gave us thousands of years of forgotten history and rich literature, these tablets ignored the history, religion and literature of its people. As Sir

Arthur Evans had suspected, they were little more than the detailed accounting records of the ancient Greeks—endless lists of sheep, volumes of oil, grain, chariot wheels.

Historians hope that somewhere, sometime, someone will turn up a Linear B text with a bit of poetry, the story of a battle, or a Gilgamesh-like tale. Although they seem terribly limited, the records on the tablets still have value. They at least reveal to us the language spoken at the time of the Trojan War. By preserving the bookkeeping of that period, they tell us about the articles people used at that time and the names attached to them, thus offering a bit of information about Bronze Age Greece.

But, without a written history, how do we know who the Minoans and Mycenaeans were? Where did they come from? How do they fit into the tapestry of the ancient world? Today, after three-quarters of a century of exploration, of sifting through archaeological and other evidence, a goodly number of authorities feel that the ancestors of the Minoans came to Crete from Asia Minor, perhaps from Syria or Anatolia, about 4000 B.C. They were Stone Age people who did not develop a high civilization. Evans believed that civilization came to Crete and other Aegean islands from the Nile Valley, shortly after the conquest of Lower Egypt by Menes around 3200 B.C. Perhaps refugees from the Nile Delta came to the Aegean islands, bringing with them their arts and advanced techniques. A possible proof of this is that the capital of the western Nile Delta before 3200 B.C., was a city called Saïs. Its people used ritual symbols—the double axe, the figure-eight shield and others—which were frequently found in Minoan and Mycenaean ruins and mentioned in Homer's epics.

The new civilization began to flourish on various Aegean islands, but by the Middle Period (1800–1450 B.C.), Knossos, on Crete, became the dominant political force. At the height of its power the Minoan Empire was destroyed, most likely by a cataclysmic volcanic explosion of the island of Thera which raised great tidal waves that swept the Aegean and Mediterranean. This vast natural upheaval followed by earthquakes, rains of volcanic ash, fire and tidal floods destroyed every city on Crete, about 1450 B.C.

But what about Schliemann's Mycenaeans? Although Evans* believed they were Minoans who had settled on the Greek mainland, most anthropologists feel that they were originally a rather primitive, hardy, warrior race that had entered Greece from the north and, in time, imitated and adopted the more advanced Minoan culture. After the destruction of Knossos, they invaded

---

* Sir Arthur Evans devised a Minoan chronology with divisions called Early, Middle and Late Minoan, and each of these was subdivided into stages I, II and III. Based on more recent discoveries and studies, Prof. N. Platon has refined and revised the chronology as follows:

Dates B.C.	Evans Periods	Revised Periods
? −2600	Early Minoan I	Neolithic
2600–2000	Early Minoan II Early Minoan III Middle Minoan I-A	Pre-palatial
2000–1700	Middle Minoan I-B Middle Minoan II	Proto-palatial
1700–1400	Middle Minoan III Late Minoan I Late Minoan II	Neo-palatial
1400–1100	Late Minoan III	Post-palatial or Mycenaean

Pre-palatial covers the period from the introduction of copper to the building of the first palaces at Knossos, Phaestos and Mallia. Post-palatial describes the period during which the palaces of Crete seem to have been deserted, and ends with the Dorian conquest.

Crete and rebuilt Knossos. This would account for Linear B tablets being found on the mainland and *only* at Knossos on Crete. From about 1450 B.C. to 1100 B.C., the Mycenaean Empire rivaled Egypt. The siege of Troy in the first quarter of the twelfth century B.C., was part of the Mycenaean campaign to control Asia Minor. This thrust was broken by Egypt's Ramses III in 1221 B.C.

18

The Next Decipherments

In this book we have described how a handful of ancient languages and their scripts were rescued from the abyss of time by curious travelers and skillful decipherers. We have not had space, however, to mention dozens of other enigmatic writings such as Germanic and Turkish runes, African scripts and forgotten Oriental writing systems, which still puzzle mankind. Some of these may never be solved. Despite the many aids which the modern decipherer can draw upon—electronic computers, new techniques of cryptanalysis, great stores of philological material and assistance from all the sciences—cracking these languages may be impossible because of insufficient texts, lack of bilinguals or perhaps, no visiting Herodotus to furnish historical clues.

Though amateur and professional scholars are still working on dozens of unsolved scripts, there are four which seem to offer the greatest challenge because we feel they might tell us more about our own heritage. These fascinating four are: the Maya hieroglyphics, the Linear A of the Minoans, the ancient signs from the Indus Valley and the Etruscan writing of Italy.

We have already described the progress being made with the writing of the ancient Maya civilization. Although the meaning of a large number of the Maya glyphs is known, the structure of the language remains a mystery. Is it a phonetic syllabary, or a combination of this and pictographs? Maya scholars no longer expect a dramatic, Champollion-like breakthrough. They are confident they will eventually understand the language, but its solution will continue to be a slow, painstaking fitting together of pieces, like assembling an enormous jigsaw puzzle.

Although we know that the Linear B script (identified as Greek and deciphered by Michael Ventris) used the same Minoan script signs as Linear A, the latter still has not been deciphered. Linear A represents an older, unknown language spoken on Crete and other Aegean islands. Scholars have found some connections between the Linear A signs of Crete and signs in the Cypriotic syllabary script. Some believe that the early Minoan of Linear A may be related to certain northwest Semitic tongues similar to Hittite. Recent evidence points to the possibility that the ancient Minoans as well as some northwest Semitic groups, including the Hebrews, may have originated in the Nile Delta, which could account for common cultural ties shared by the Minoans, Phoenicians, early Greeks and Hebrews.

One of the oldest, unsolved language puzzles in Europe is posed by the language and script of the ancient Etruscans who shaped the first high civilization in Italy. The Etruscans used an alphabet. Their alphabet can be read, yet no one has been able to reconstruct their language. It is a strange situation because the Etruscan civilization flourished at the same time as the Greek, it was in contact with the Phoenicians, and much of it was absorbed into the Roman civilization. Although countless examples of Etruscan writing have been found, with few exceptions these have been very short epigraphs taken from grave markers. They offer the decipherer scarcely more help than if he tried to reconstruct English from tombstones having little more on them than, "Here lies John Doe, son of Ed and Martha, b. January 10, 1912, d. December 10, 1962." The briefness of these epigraphs, and the lack of any Greek, Phoenician or Roman bilinguals, has greatly hindered the unraveling of the language of a highly artistic people.

A fourth system of writing which has intrigued scholars throughout the world is a script found on a large number of seals and small copper plates uncovered in the impressive mound ruins at Harappa in the Punjab region of India, and at Mohenjo-Daro in the Indus River delta. Excavation of the mounds during this century has uncovered the remains of an extensive, mysterious civilization that flourished as far back as the second millennium B.C. This civilization may have had cultural or trade ties with the people of Mesopotamia, for some of their curious seals have been found in Sumerian excavations.

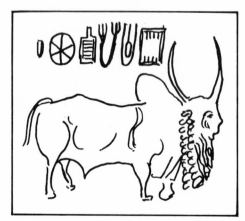

Indus Valley seal signs or script.

Indus Valley seal.

Until recently the Indus Valley script has resisted decipherment. Some two hundred or more signs have been identified, an indication that the writing was picto-ideographic rather then alphabetic or syllabic. But working out the meaning of the signs has been difficult because no tablets or long texts have been found. Nevertheless, scholars seem to be making some progress; Prof. Piero Meriggi, using the same grid technique developed by Alice Kober and Michael Ventris for their attack on Linear B, has made tentative decipherments.

An amusing but highly improbable attempt to link the Indus Valley script with a curious writing found on Easter Island in the Pacific was made by W. Von Hevesy, a German student of calligraphy. The old script, called *rongo rongo* ("the speaking wood"), was preserved on wooden tablets that were first discovered in the 1870s. Although none of the modern inhabitants of the remote island could read the writing, Bishop Jaussen of Tahiti began collecting the "talking boards." The signs on them were most puzzling because, unlike any known scripts, the alternate lines seemed to be written upside down.

Jaussen, after a good deal of searching, located a young Easter Islander named Metoro who claimed he could read the tablets. Actually, he chanted the lines while the good bishop wrote down the sounds as best he could. Jaussen then made a French translation which did not always make sense. The scene reminds one of Bishop Landa of Yucatán recording the "reading" of Indian informants who no longer knew how to read the Maya glyphs. And again, history repeated itself; for many years the bishop's manuscript was forgotten on archive shelves in Rome.

Meanwhile, working with the few samples of the Easter Island tablets to reach European museums, Von Hevesy put together an interesting chart of forty-eight *rongo rongo* signs and the same number of similar looking Indus Valley signs. He claimed this was proof that the two scripts were related.

Ten of Von Hevesy comparisons between the Indus Valley and Easter Island scripts.

Indus Valley

Easter Island

Serious scholars rejected his "proof." The reasons were obvious. First, the valley of the Indus River and Easter Island are as far apart as two geographic areas can be. It was almost as if a forgotten civilization at the South Pole somehow conveyed its writing system to another civilization at the North Pole. Second, the two cultures stood just as far apart in time, a gap of almost four thousand years separating them. Third, Von Hevesy selected only about a sixth of the signs from each script for his comparison, ignoring the hundreds of other signs that were not alike. In most cases the signs he selected were universal signs which have been used over and over by unrelated cultures since man first began to write. These included wavy lines to represent water, circles to symbolize the sun, a stick figure to stand for man.

In 1954 a young German ethnologist, Thomas Barthel, rerouted *rongo rongo* studies from such fanciful flights back to the world of serious decipherment. He located Bishop Jaussen's forgotten manuscript as well as copies of the script from various European and American museums. Barthel and other specialists feel the Easter island writing is not a language system in the same

210

sense as English or ancient Egyptian. It is, rather, a grouping of mnemonic signs (memory ticklers) used by the ancestors of the present-day Easter Islanders to help memorize ritual chants. Dr. Barthel, however, seems to have made some progress in interpreting some of the chants. If the direction he has taken is correct, his decipherments may not recover a lost language, but they may reveal something about the origins of the islanders.

Professional scholars, especially anthropologists, are often suspicious of new concepts dealing with cultural diffusion. The term *cultural diffusion* is frequently used for a situation in which a civilization may be influenced by cultural contributions from another people living a vast distance away. Scholars are most suspicious in cases where the transfer may be accidental. For example, a Chinese junk is caught in a violent storm and is blown to the coast of Mexico about the year 500 A.D. The sailors settle in the new country, passing on a few of their crafts and techniques to the natives, who incorporate them in their cultural baggage. Situations such as this may have occurred, but anthropologists are uncertain of how important the cultural impact may have been. The reason for their caution is that overenthusiastic individuals too often soar off on flights of fancy, such as Von Hevesy's Easter Island–Indus Valley theory, without supporting their idea with additional evidence.

But occasionally serious scholars will indulge in almost similar flights. It is done, however, to stir up interest, to suggest new avenues of investigation, to elicit a constructive or critical response from other scholars. In the preface of this book such a situation was mentioned; two distinguished professors entertaining the idea what there might be some "script connection" between ancient people of the Near East and American Indians.

This fascinating story is worth retelling. It began at Fort Benning, Georgia, where a man named Manfred Metcalf found a stone with strange signs inscribed on it while he was constructing a barbecue pit. He turned the stone over to Joseph B. Mahan, Jr., a specialist in American Indian archaeology and ethnology at the Museum of Arts and Crafts in Columbus, Georgia. Mahan thought the inscribed stone might be remotely related to the Yuchi Indians who had lived in Georgia until 1836, when they had been exiled to Oklahoma. The Yuchis were racially and linguistically different from other Indians. Mahan was intrigued by a curious Yuchi harvest festival during which, for eight days, the Indians lived in roofless booths covered with foliage and fruits. During the festival they also circled a fire and during these processions they carried branches which they shook vigorously. The ritual seemed quite like the ancient Hebrew Feast of the Booths (Sukkoth).

In 1968 Mahan sent a cast of the Metcalf Stone to Dr. Cyrus H. Gordon of Brandeis University. Professor Gordon is an outstanding authority on Semitic languages and culture, as well as being one of the scholars most involved in the study of the Linear A script and other Aegean syllabaries. Although Dr. Gordon seemed to find no linguistic connection between Yuchi words, the Metcalf Stone, and any language he knew, nevertheless, he spotted affinities between Minoan signs and the symbols on the stone.

In 1970 he showed a cast of the Metcalf Stone to Stanislav Segert of the University of Prague, Czechoslovakia. Segert, an internationally renowned professor of Semitic languages, identified the signs on the stone as an Aegean script from about the second milennium B.C., a period when the Aegean peoples were slowly shifting from a syllabic type of writing to an alphabetic system.

The stone, of course, might be a prankster's forgery, similar

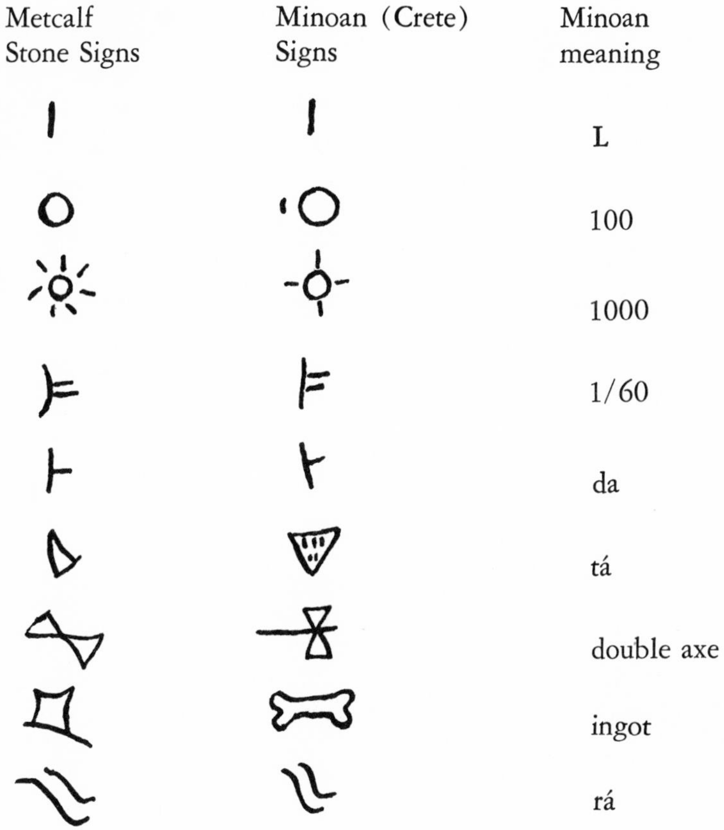
Metcalf Stone Signs
Minoan (Crete) Signs
Minoan meaning
L
100
1000
1/60
da
tá
double axe
ingot
rá

(Courtesy, *Manuscripts*)

Grody's comparison of signs in Crete's Phaistos Disc with Aztec glyphs.

Aztec Signs
Minoan Signs

(Courtesy, *Manuscripts*)

to the Kensington Stone with its Norse runic script which was found in Minnesota. Then, again, the Metcalf Stone might not be part of a hoax, though no one can yet say how it came to be in Georgia. It does seem to be part of a mystifying riddle, because a short while after Dr. Segert related the stone's signs to an Aegean script, another well-known linguist, Magnus Grodys of Norway, called the scientific world's attention to similarities between some Aztec glyphs and signs engraved on the Minoan Phaistos Stone.*

These and other fascinating "evidences"—for example, the recent discovery of the papyrus plant, a native of Egypt, growing in the wilds of southeast Mexico—were not offered as proof of a transoceanic cultural diffusion. These have simply been put forth as materials worth further investigation.

It is this sort of open-mindedness and intellectual curiosity, plus scholarly dedication, which has produced a succession of brilliant decipherers who, in turn, have helped revolutionize the humanities. Their work on forgotten scripts has not been mere academic exercises or puzzle-solving games. Language and, above all, writing distinguishes men from beasts. Writing preserves the very essence of the mind. The ability to bring it back to life, to maintain its health, is as important as the surgeon's skill in administering to the human heart or the psychologist's knowledge of the human personality.

In this book we have explored a few notable decipherments. We have seen, to some extent, how the men who solve the

* The story of the Metcalf Stone and other tantalizing mysteries concerning contacts between the old and new world are fully covered in Dr. Cyrus H. Gordon's book *Riddles in History* (New York: Crown Publishers, Inc., 1973).

enigma of forgotten scripts also make our heritage more understandable and meaningful. Although the nineteenth century was called the great age of decipherments, there are still unsolved systems of writing to challenge future Champollions and Youngs, Grotefends and Rawlinsons. There are still hidden treasures awaiting a future Niebuhr or Evans. There are missing literatures which may yet be recovered, literatures of the Etruscans, of the Khmers of Cambodia, of the Phoenicians of Tyre and Sidon, of the Carthaginians and of the Numidians.

Chronology

Dates B.C.	EGYPT	NEAR EAST AND ASIA
4000	Late Neolithic and early Copper Age Settlement of the Nile Valley	c. 3200. Predynastic Sumerian cities begun
3000	Egyptian Dynasties I and II Menes unites Upper and Lower Egypt	Early dynasties of Kish, Erech, Ur, in Mesopotamia
2700	**Old Kingdom** Dynasty III, Zoser	
2500	Dynasty IV, Khufu (Cheops) great pyramid at Giza	Cities of Harappa and Mohenjo-Daro in the Indus Valley
2400	Dynasties V–VI	
2300	**First Interlude** Dynasties VII to X	Dynasty of Akkad, 2360–2300 Sargon, 2360–2305 2300–2200 Ur supreme in Mesopotamia 2150 Third Dynasty of Ur
2100	**Middle Kingdom** Amenemhet I Dynasty XI Sesostris I	Great ziggurat at Ur constructed In the north the kings of Assur (Assyria) begin to play major role

2050 Ilu-Shuman of Assur rules in the north

Kassite Dynasties rule northern Mesopotamia (Babylon-Assyria) 1775–1150

Hittites conquer Babylon
Early Assyrian Empire
(1380–1093)
Tiglath-pileser I (1115–1093)

Second Dynasty of Ur (1170–1039, controlled southern Mesopotamia. Nebuchadnezzar, 1146–1143

Hittite kingdom destroyed by sea-people

Assyrians conquer Babylon

Late Assyrian Empire
Assyrian, Elamite, Chaldean rule 990–625
Assurnasirpal, 885–859
Tiglath-pileser III
Sargon II
Assurbanipal, 668–626

Sesostris II
Amenemhet III

Dynasties XII
Second Interlude
Dynasties XIII–XVII (including the Hyksos or Asiatic invaders)

New Kingdom
Hatshepsut
Dynasty XVIII Thothmes III
(1555–1335) Amenhotep III
Amenhotep IV
Tutankhamen

Dynasty XIX Ramses II
Dynasty XX Ramses III

Third Interlude
Dynasties XXI–XXIV (1090–712)

2000
1900
1800

1600

1200

1100

1000

900

800

Dates B.C.	EGYPT	NEAR EAST AND ASIA
700	Late Period, Dynasty XXV. Kushites conquer Upper Egypt	
	Assyrian rule over Egypt, 663–525	Chaldean Dynasty Nebuchadnezzar II (604–562)
600		**Persian Empire** Cyrus (559–529), Cambyses (529–522) Darius I (521–485), Xerxes (485–464) Darius II and III (424–330) Behistun Rock inscribed
	Persian rule over Egypt, 525–330	
500	Herodotus tours Egypt, Kush, the Near East	
300	**Hellenistic Period** Alexander the Great conquers Egypt in 332 Ptolemy I establishes dynasty, 304	**Hellenistic Period** Alexander invades Persia, conquers Persepolis, 330
200	Rosetta Stone inscribed, 196	Rome expands into Middle East
100	Romans conquer Egypt, 31 Cleopatra and Marc Antony commit suicide	
0		

A.D.

Jesus Christ born
Rome conquers Mesopotamia, 60 A.D.

400   Horapollon

600

700   Beginning of the Moslem era

1000   Bagdad University founded
Genghis Khan, Mongul Empire, 1200
Ottoman Dynasty in Turkey, 1290

1300

1500

Dates B.C.	EUROPE	MESOAMERICA
		Early hunters, 20,000–1000 B.C. Tepexpán Man, c. 12,000–10,000
4000	Neolithic Period	
		Archaic Cultures Chalco Industries (pottery) and Chupícuaro culture
3000	Early Minoan I (Bronze Age culture in the Aegean)	
2700	Early Helladic (Bronze Age culture on Greek mainland)	
2500	Early Minoan II	
2400	Middle Helladic	
2300	Early Minoan III, cities on Crete	
2100	Middle Minoan I Middle Helladic	
2000	Middle Minoan II	
1900		
1800	Middle Minoan III **Late Helladic I** (Early Mycenaean) Late Minoan I (peak of Minoan culture)	

Formative Period–Pre-Classic
(1500 B.C.–A.D. 200)

Beginnings of ceremonial centers
Tlaltilco, Olmec and Zapotec cultures

1600	Late Minoan II. (Stonehenge in Britain)
	Late Helladic II (Middle Mycenaean) Minoan culture ends abruptly, 1450
1300	Late Helladic III and Late Mycenaean
1200	Trojan War Etruscans invade central Italy
1100	Doric migrations
1000	**Greek Antiquity**
900	
800	**Greek Middle Period** Rise of Greek city-states Homer
700	First Olympiad (c. 776)
600	Persian Wars

Dates
B.C.

Dates B.C.	EUROPE	MESOAMERICA
500	Persian forces defeated at Thermopylae and Salamis, 480 Golden Age of Athens Herodotus tours Egypt and Near East	
300	Peloponnesian War (431–404)	
	Hellenistic Age Alexander the Great (336–323) Rome begins rise to power	
200	Rome conquers Greece	**Florescent Period** (200 B.C.–A.D. 600)
100	Julius Caesar assassinated	Rise of Teotihuacan culture, central Mexico Totonac culture, Gulf Coast Nayarit and Colima cultures, west coast Zapotec culture, southern Mexico Maya (Old Empire), Yucatán, Chiapas, Guatemala
0 A.D.		
400	Vandals sack Rome	

600	Mongols invade Europe	**Fusional Period** Toltecs rise to power, central Mexico Maya Empire at its peak
700	Moslems conquer Spain	Maya Empire declines
1000	Norman invasion of England, 1066 First Crusade, 1096	Toltecs and central Mexicans occupy Maya cities in Yucatán (987–1204)
1300	Hundred Years' War begins	**Militarist Period** Aztecs begin rise to power, found Tenochtitlán (1325)
1500		Spanish Conquest begins, 1519

Bibliography

For the reader or student seeking more detailed and specialized accounts of the development of writing and decipherment of ancient languages, books listed under GENERAL WORKS are especially recommended. Other books, manuscripts and journals consulted for this work are subdivided according to subjects; that is, all references dealing with the decipherment of Egyptian writing are entered under that heading. Titles and authors listed under one heading will not be repeated under another. For example, although Carsten Niebuhr was involved in the recovery of both Egyptian hieroglyphics and Persian cuneiforms, his work is mentioned only once—under the first subject heading, EGYPTIAN SCRIPTS.

General Works

Arago, F. *Biographies of Distinguished Scientific Men.* London: Longman, Brown, Green, Longman & Roberts, 1957.

Ceram, C. W. *Gods, Graves and Scholars.* New York: Alfred A. Knopf, 1951.

Cleator, P. E. *Lost Languages.* New York: John Day, 1959.

Deuel, Leo. *Testaments of Time.* London: Secker & Warburg, 1966.

————. *The Treasures of Time.* Cleveland, Ohio: World Publishing Co., 1961.

Doblhofer, Ernst. *Voices in Stone.* New York: Viking, 1961.

Encyclopedia Britannica.

Friedrich, Johannes. *Extinct Languages.* New York: Philosophical Library, 1957.

Gordon, Cyrus H. *Forgotten Scripts.* London: Thames & Hudson, 1968.

Jensen, Hans. *Sign, Symbol and Script.* New York: Putnam's Sons, 1969.

Kahn, David. *The Codebreakers.* New York: MacMillan, 1967.

Kenyon, F. G. *The Bible and Archaeology.* London: George Harrap, 1940.

Marshack, Alexander. *The Roots of Civilization.* New York: McGraw-Hill, 1972.

Schlaugh, Margaret. *The Gift of Tongues.* New York: Modern Age, 1932.

Egyptian Scripts

Aldred, Cyril. *The Egyptians.* London: Thames & Hudson, 1968.

Belzoni, Giovanni B. *Narrative of the Operations and Recent Discoveries within the Pyramids, Temples, Tombs and Excavations in Egypt and Nubia.* London: John Murray, 1820.

Bruce, James. *Travels to Discover the Source of the Nile in the Years 1768–72.* Edinburgh: G. G. T. & J. Robinson, 1790.

Budge, Ernest A. W. *The Book of the Dead.* 3 vols. New York: Putnam's Sons, 1913.

————. *The Rosetta Stone.* London: British Museum, 1913.

Champollion, Jean François. *Lettre à M. Dacier, relative à l'alphabet des hiéroglyphes phonétiques.* Paris, 1822.

Champollion-Figeac, Amié. *Les Deux Champollion: Leur Vie et Leurs Oeuvres.* Grenoble: Libraire de l'Acadámie, 1887.

Denon, Dominique Vivant. *Travels in Upper and Lower Egypt.* New York: Heard & Forman, 1803.

Frankfort, Henri. *The Birth of Civilization in the Near East.* New York: Doubleday Anchor, 1956.

Hartleben, H. *Champollion.* 2 vols. Berlin: Weidmann, 1906.

Herodotus. *Histories.* Translated by H. C. Rawlinson. New York: Everyman, E. P. Dutton & Co., 1964.

Horapollon. *Hieroglyphics.* Translated by George Boas. New York: Bollingen Series, Pantheon Press, 1950.

Niebuhr, Carsten. *Travels through Arabia.* 2 vols. London: R. Morison & Son, 1892.

Oldham, F. *Sir Thomas Young.* London: Arnold, 1933.

Pourpont, Madelaine. *Champollion et l'enigme Ègyptienne.* Paris: Cercle Français des Livres.

Wood, A. *Thomas Young, Natural Philosopher.* Cambridge, England: Cambridge University Press, 1954.

Cuneiforms of Persia, Babylonia and Sumeria

Botta, Paul E. *Monuments de Ninive découverts et décrits par Botta, mesurés et dessinés par E. Flandin.* 5 vols. Paris, 1847–1850.

Budge, Ernest A. W. *The Rise and Progress of Assyriology.* London: Martin Hopkinson & Co., 1925.

Chardin, John. *Sir John Chardin: Travels in Persia.* London: Argonaut Press, 1927.

Gordon, Cyrus H. *The Ancient Near East.* New York: Norton, 1965.

Kubie, Nora B. *The Road to Nineveh.* London, 1965.

Layard, Austen Henry. *Nineveh and Its Remains.* New York: Putnam's Sons, 1949.

Rawlinson, Henry Creswicke. *A Commentary on the Cuneiform Inscriptions of Babylon and Assyria.* London: British Museum, 1850.

————. *The Persian Cuneiform Inscriptions at Behistun.* London: British Museum, 1870–1884.

Sacy, Silvestre de. *Mémoires sur diverses Antiquités de Perse.* Paris: Imprimerie Nationale, 1793.

Smith, George. *Assyrian Discoveries.* London: Sampson, Low, Marston, Low & Searle, 1885.

————. *A Chaldean Account of the Deluge.* Transaction of the Society of Biblical Archaeology, vol. II. July 1873.

Speiser, E. A. *The Epic of Gilgamesh.* Translated in *Ancient Near Eastern Texts.* Princeton, N.J.: Princeton University Press, 1950.

Wooley, C. Leonard. *Excavations at Ur.* London: Penguin Books, 1926.

Hittite, Ugaritic and Others

Bauer, H. *Das Alphabet von Ras Schamra.* Halle: Niemeyer Verlag, 1932.

Burckhardt, Johann L. *Travels in Syria and the Holy Land.* London: Royal Geographical Society, 1822.

Dhorme, Édouard. *Le déchiffrement des tablettes de Ras Schamra; Recueil Édouard Dhorme.* Paris: Imprimerie Nationale, 1951.

Gelb, I. J. *Hittite Hieroglyphics.* 3 vols. Chicago: Chicago University Press, 1931–1942.

Mercer, S. A. *The Tell el-Amarna Tablets.* Toronto: Macmillan, 1939.

Sayce, Archibald Henry. *Reminiscences.* London: Macmillan & Co., 1923.

Schaeffer, Claude. *The Cuneiform Texts of Ras Shamra-Ugarit.*
Oxford: British Academy-Oxford University Press, 1939.
————. "Discoveries at Ras Shamara." *Illustrated London News,*
November 29, 1930.
————. "A New Alphabet of the Ancients Is Unearthed." *National Geographic Magazine,* October 1930.

The New World Scripts

Bernal, Ignacio. *Mexico before Cortés: Art, History, Legend.* New
York: Doubleday Dolphin, 1963.
Brinton, Daniel G. "The Abbé Brasseur de Bourbourg and His
Labors." *Lippincott's Magazine,* January 1868.
————. *The Maya Chronicles.* Philadelphia: Brinton's Library
of Aboriginal American Literature, no. 1, 1882.
Caso, Alfonso. *The Aztecs: People of the Sun.* Norman, Okla.:
University of Oklahoma Press, 1950.
Covarribias, Miguel. *Indian Art of Mexico and Central America.*
New York: Alfred Knopf, 1957.
Días del Castillo, Bernal. *The Discovery and Conquest of Mexico,
1519–21.* Translated by A. P. Maudslay. New York: Farrar,
Strauss & Cudahy, 1956.
Haven, Samuel. *Notes on Alexander Humboldt and His Service
to American Archaeology.* American Antiquarian Society,
Proceedings, no. 70, 1878.
Humboldt, Alexander von. *Researches Concerning the Institutions and Monuments of the Ancient Inhabitants of America,
with Descriptions and Views of Some of the Most Striking
Scenes in the Cordilleras.* 2 vols. London: Longsman, 1814.
Kingsborough, Edward K. *Antiquities of Mexico.* 9 vols. London:
R. Havell (vols. 1–7) and H. G. Bohn (vols. 8–9) 1831–
1848.
Landa, Diego de. *Relación de las Cosas de Yucatán.* Translated
by A. M. Tozzer. Cambridge, Mass.: The Peabody Museum,
Harvard University, 1941.

Morley, Sylvanus G. *The Ancient Maya.* Stanford, Calif.: Stanford University Press, 1946.

Norman, James. *Terry's Guide to Mexico.* New York: Doubleday & Co., 1972.

Prescott, William H. *The History of the Conquest of Mexico.* New York: Modern Library.

Proskouriakoff, Tatiana. "Historical Data in the Inscriptions of Yaxchilán." *Estudios de Cultura Maya,* Mexico, no. 3, 1963–1964.

————. "Historical Implications of a Pattern of Dates at Piedras Negras, Guatemala." *American Antiquity,* no. 25. Salt Lake, 1960.

————. "The Lords of the Maya Realm." *Expedition,* vol. IV, no. 1, Fall 1961.

Robertson, Donald. *Mexican Manuscript Painting of the Early Colonial Period.* New Haven, Conn.: Yale University Press, 1959.

Stephens, John L. *Incidents of Travel in Central America, Chiapas and Yucatán.* Rutgers, N. J.: Rutgers University Press, 1949.

Thompson, J. Eric S. *The Civilization of the Mayas.* Chicago: Chicago Natural History Museum Press, 1958.

Valliant, George. *The Aztecs of Mexico.* New York: Doubleday & Co., 1962.

Wauchope, Robert. *Lost Tribes and Sunken Continents: Myths and Methods in the Study of American Indians.* Chicago: Chicago University Press, 1962.

Minoan, Mycenaean and Cypriotic Scripts

Blegen, Carl W. *Troy.* Cincinnati, O. and Princeton, N.J.: University of Cincinnati Press and Princeton University Press, 1950.

Brice, W. C. *Inscriptions in the Minoan Linear Script of Class A.* New York: Oxford University Press, 1961.

Chadwick, John. *The Decipherment of Linear B.* 2d ed. Cambridge: Cambridge University Press, 1970.

Evans, Sir Arthur. *The Palace of Minos.* London: Macmillan, 1921–1935.

———. *Scripta Minoa I.* Oxford: Oxford University Press, 1909.

Evans, Joan. *Time and Chance.* London: Longman, Green, 1943.

Gordon, Cyrus H. *Evidence for the Minoan Language.* Ventnor, N.J.: Ventnor Press, 1966.

Homer. *The Iliad* and *The Odyssey.* Translated by W. H. D. Rouse. New York: New American Library (Mentor), 1950.

Ludwig, Emil. *Schliemann of Troy.* New York: Putnam's Sons, 1931.

Myres, Sir John L. *Who Were the Greeks?* Berkeley and Los Angeles: University of California Press, 1931.

Ventris, Michael, and Chadwick, John. *Documents in Mycenaean Greek.* London: Cambridge University Press, 1956.

Wace, Allan. *Mycenae.* Princeton, N.J.: Princeton University Press, 1949.

The Next Decipherments

Davis, S. *The Phaistos Disc and the Eteocretan Inscriptions from Psychro and Praisos.* Johannesburg: Witwaterstrand University Press, 1961.

Gordon, Cyrus H. *Riddles in History.* New York: Crown, 1973.

Hevesi, M. G. de. "Easter Island and Indus Valley Scripts." *Orientalist Journal,* no. 11, 1934.

Heyerdahl, Thor. *Aku-Aku.* New York: Rand-McNally, 1958.

Hunter, G. R. *The Script of Harappa and Mohenjodaro.* London: Kegan Paul, Trench, Trubner & Co., 1934.

MacKay, E. J. *Excavations at Mohenjo-Daro.* Delhi: 1938.

Marshall, John. *Mohenjo-Daro and the Indus Civilization.* 3 vols. London: MacKay, Lovat, Dickson & Thompson Ltd., 1935.

Metraux, A. *Easter Island.* New York: Oxford University Press, 1957.

Pallottino, M. *The Etruscans.* London: Pelican Books, 1956.

Index

Abu Simbel, 61
Achaemenian Dynasty, 71, 76, 79, 82, 83
Aglio, Agostino, 141, 142
Åkerblad, David, 43, 44, 48, 63
Akkadians, 67, 81, 82, 83, 108, 118, 125
  script of, 104, 105, 129
Aleppo, 114, 115
Alexander the Great, 5
Alexandria, Egypt, 25, 27, 30, 41
alphabetic languages, 12, 19, 72, 137, 163
Altamira cave paintings, 8
amatl, 136
Amorite nomads, 83
Anatolians, 13, 199
  and writing, 13
The Annals of Cakchiquels, 155
The Annals of Cuauhtitlán, 155, 166

Anquetil-Duperron, Abraham Hyacinthe, 71, 72
Antiquities of Mexico, 146, 148
Arabian Nights, 69, 102
Aramaeans, 83
Aryans, 8
Arzawa script, 123, 125, 128
Assyrian-Babylonian cuneiforms, 3, 104
Assyrians, 83, 116
Assyrian Discoveries, 114
Aswan, Egypt, 26
Athenaeus, 66
Athens, 182
Aubin, J. M., 161
Aztecs, 134, 136, 139, 150, 155, 162, 163
  writing of, 153, 162
  interpretation of codices, 158–59

Moctezuma, 135, 140
Mohenjo-Daro, 208
Morley, Sylvanius, 155, 166, 168
Mosul, 100, 101, 102, 103, 110, 114
Motul Dictionary, 155
Mount Elvend, 86, 87
Münden, Germany, 74
Münter, Christian Earl, 72, 76
    word separators, 72
Mycenaeans, 187, 189, 203, 204
Myres, Sir John, 191, 200
    Scripta Minoa II, 191

Nahuatl, 138, 161
Naqsh-e-Rustam, 69, 76
Naranjo, 174, 175
A Narrative of a Journey to the Site of Babylon, 100
National Museum of Anthropology, Mexico, 4
Nelson, Admiral Lord, 30
Neolithic Era, 5, 187
Niebuhr, Carsten, 27, 28, 29, 30, 33, 38, 70, 72, 75, 79, 215
    on decipherment, 28–29
    early years, 27
    and modern Egyptology, 27
    in Persepolis, 70
    Travels in Arabia and Other Countries, 28
Nineveh, 67, 94, 96, 101, 102, 103, 107, 109, 110, 113, 114
Nineveh and Its Remains, 103
Nippur, 110, 116
Norris, Edwin, 93, 105, 131
Numidian, 119, 133, 215
Nuttall, Zelia, 161

obelisks, 32, 33, 44
Odyssey, 78, 193
Olmecas, 168
Omar, Caliph, 23
Oppert, Jules, 105, 106, 107, 108, 109, 110
    phonetic system of Old Persian, 108
Orientalists, 26, 36, 38, 71, 75, 81, 85, 87, 101, 107

Palace of Minos, 191
Palace of Sennacherib, 103
Palaian, 119, 132
Palenque, 150, 153, 175
Parsees, 71
Parthians, 72
Peabody Museum, 7, 172, 174
Pehlevi, 42, 72
Persepolis, 67, 68, 69, 70
petroglyphs, 8
petrograms, 8
    Altamira cave paintings, 8
Phoenicians, 215
phonetic script, 163
pictograms, 8, 9, 10, 11, 36, 61, 139
    faults as writing system, 10
Piedras Negras, 174, 175
pithoi, 185
polyphonous signs, 104
Pope Sixtus V, 36
Pope Urban VIII, 25
Proskouriakoff, Tatiana, 174
Prescott, William H., 152, 153, 166
    The Conquest of Mexico, 153
Ptolemy, 40, 43, 44, 45, 46

Quechua, 138